"At last we have a comprehensive treatment of the sad history of the Vatican's dismantling of ICEL's efforts at providing us with translations that are both elegant and communicative. My favorite line: 'Before I die, I would be delighted to celebrate once again the Eucharist in my native language.' This book provides trenchant criticism of the current translation of the Roman Missal and wonderful observations on the 1998 'Missal that wasn't.' As in so many areas of contemporary theology, we are once again in O'Collins's debt."

—John F. Baldovin, SJ
  Professor of Historical and Liturgical Theology
  Boston College School of Theology & Ministry

"Authoritative, well detailed, and searingly honest, this account of the recent history of Vatican translation policy and its devastating effect on the current English version of the *Roman Missal* needs to be read by any liturgy scholar, teacher, or presider who uses these texts or, indeed, tries to explain them. O'Collins and Wilkins bring a wealth of experience and insight into the story of the process, the high quality of the 1998 material, and the most evident problems and contradictions in the texts that English-speaking Catholics hear and repeat every Sunday.

"The timing of this publication, as it happens, could not have been better. The role of the bishops in taking primary responsibility for the liturgical texts authorized for use in their own countries and linguistic communities is now consistent with that envisioned at Vatican II. New reasons for hope for a truly vernacular and participative liturgy."

—Susan Roll
  Saint Paul University
  Ottawa, Canada

"Here is a required book for any class in contemporary Roman Catholic eucharistic liturgy today. O'Collins narrates the rise and fall of the 1998 ICEL translation of the Roman Missal and its replacement by the 2010 'translation.' Together with ample references to the best in contemporary liturgical scholarship and official documents—including *Comme le prevoit* and *Liturgiam authenticam*—O'Collins calls for the end of the 2010 text with its impossible syntax and forced 'sacral language' in favor of an official recognition of the 1998 text. With serious ecumenical implications as well (especially with regard to what were common texts of the *Kyrie, Gloria,* Creed, *Sanctus,* and *Agnus Dei*), this book needs to be read by all in light of Pope Francis's call for a reevaluation of *Liturgiam authenticam.* May O'Collins's hope be realized and may the 2010 text become but a footnote in the history of the Roman Rite."

—Maxwell E. Johnson
University of Notre Dame

LOST IN TRANSLATION
The English Language and the Catholic Mass

Gerald O'Collins
with
John Wilkins

LITURGICAL PRESS
ACADEMIC

Collegeville, Minnesota
www.litpress.org

Cover design by Monica Bokinskie.
Photo courtesy of Catholic News Service/Nancy Phelan Wiechec.
Used with permission.

1   2   3   4   5   6   7   8   9

Library of Congress Cataloging-in-Publication Data

Names: O'Collins, Gerald, author.
Title: Lost in translation : the English language and the Catholic Mass / Gerald O'Collins, with John Wilkins.
Description: Collegeville, Minnesota : Liturgical Press, 2017. | Includes bibliographical references and index.
Identifiers: LCCN 2017024757 (print) | LCCN 2017036508 (ebook) | ISBN 9780814644812 (ebooks) | ISBN 9780814644577
Subjects: LCSH: Catholic Church. Missale Romanum (1970)—Translations into English—History and criticism. | Liturgical language—English. | Catholic Church—Liturgy—Texts—History and criticism. | Catholic Church. Congregatio de Cultu Divino et Disciplina Sacramentorum. Liturgiam authenticam.
Classification: LCC BX2015.25 (ebook) | LCC BX2015.25 .O26 2017 (print) | DDC 264/.020014—dc23
LC record available at https://lccn.loc.gov/2017024757

Contents

Authors' Note

The history of ICEL's rise and fall in Chapter 1 is by John Wilkins. The comparative analysis of the Missals of 1998 and 2010 in the following chapters is by Gerald O'Collins. The whole book has been edited by Wilkins.

Preface

"There is only the fight to recover what has been lost."
T. S. Eliot, *East Coker*

Each week I celebrate the Eucharist for a group of old Italian men and women. It is a great joy to use a missal that sounds like good, contemporary Italian and communicates very well to my small congregation. During the rest of the week, however, I say Mass in what its translators have called a "sacred vernacular"—a language that falls halfway between Latin and English.

This sacred vernacular with which the English-speaking churches were saddled in Advent 2011 asks me to prefer "charity" over "love," "compunction" over "repentance," "laud" over "praise," "supplication" over "prayer," and "wondrous" over "wonderful." In the Creed "consubstantial with the Father" has replaced the user-friendly "of one being with the Father." At the feast of the Immaculate Conception, I am expected to talk of the "prevenient" grace that preserved Mary from all sin. Every now and then I have to speak about the eucharistic "oblation," and wonder how many of the assembled faithful think that I have mispronounced "ablution."

Before launching into some prayers, I need to take a deep breath. I face long sentences that belong more to the Latin of Cicero than to contemporary English.

Worse still, this strange new Missal wants me in the name of Jesus to declare that his blood was "poured out for you and for many," as if he did not die for all. It calls on me persistently to use a language of "merit," which moves close to the ancient heresy derived from Pelagius. Pelagius held that through our own efforts we can gain salvation. I find it distressing to read texts that encourage a "do-it-yourself" redemption.

Before I die, I would be delighted to celebrate once again the Eucharist in my native language. Hence I welcomed with delight the decision Pope Francis took just before Christmas 2016. He has appointed a commission to revisit the guidelines for translation, called *Liturgiam Authenticam* ("Authentic Liturgy"), which stood behind and "justified" the Latin words transposed into the so-called English of the present Missal. May that commission quickly propose repealing *Liturgiam Authenticam*! And may it press on to endorse the "missal that never was," an excellent translation that the Vatican summarily rejected in 1998.

The roots of the problem go back to the time of the Second Vatican Council (1962–65). In *Sacrosanctum Concilium* (the Constitution on the Sacred Liturgy, December 4, 1963), the council acknowledged that the primary responsibility in revising the liturgy for the Roman Rite belonged to the Holy See (that is to say, to the pope and his collaborators in the Vatican) *and* to the bishops of different regions (SC 22, 37–40). The same document allowed the use of vernacular translations and expected the bishops around the world to "approve" the "translations from the Latin for use in the liturgy" (SC 36.4). The council made no explicit mention of any further obligation to have these translations (into Chinese, English, French, German, Hindi, Maori, Spanish, and so forth) also confirmed or "recognized" by the Holy See. However, such an express obligation surfaced soon enough.

On January 25, 1964, Pope Paul VI issued *Sacram Liturgiam*, a *motu proprio* or personal edict that prescribed submitting translations to the Holy See for an official *recognitio* or approval.[1] When the revised *Missale Romanum*, the authorized Latin version sometimes called "the Paul VI Missal," appeared in 1970, conferences of bishops around the world were to prepare editions in the vernacular. But these editions

---

[1] For this *motu proprio*, see ICEL, *Documents on the Liturgy 1963–1979: Conciliar, Papal, and Curial Texts* (Collegeville, MN: Liturgical Press, 1982), 84–87, at 86.

would come into force only after being confirmed by the Holy See. By 1972, the International Commission on English in the Liturgy (ICEL) had finished its translation of the 1970 Roman Missal. The eleven bishops' conferences who were full members of ICEL approved the translation, the Holy See gave the required confirmation, and by 1973 the Missal was ready to be printed and distributed.

In 1981, ICEL set itself to revise painstakingly the 1972 translation and in the early 1990s submitted to the bishops' conferences segments of the revised text. All eleven English-speaking conferences approved the new translation and in 1998 submitted it to Rome for approval. Instead of discussing the text with the episcopal conferences or with ICEL, however, the prefect of the Congregation for Divine Worship and the Discipline of the Sacraments, Cardinal Medina Estévez, rejected the 1998 Missal.

Cardinal Medina demanded widespread changes in the mandate, structures, and personnel of ICEL, which led in 2003 to new statutes governing its operation. The *recognitio* of translations, enjoined by Paul VI in *Sacram Liturgiam*, ceased to be a merely formal confirmation and became an exercise of governance by the Holy See. Rome seized control of ICEL and now planned to supervise strictly this commission set up by the English-speaking conferences of bishops to prepare vernacular translations for their local churches.

ICEL was dismantled, the chairman from 1997 to 2002, Bishop Maurice Taylor of Galloway in Scotland, replaced, and a new membership installed, with key roles to be played by Bishop (later Archbishop) Arthur Roche, chairman of ICEL from 2002 to 2012, and Father (later Monsignor) Bruce Harbert. From 2002 to 2009 Harbert would be the executive director of the secretariat of the new ICEL. His appointment paralleled the establishment of the *Vox Clara* ("Clear Voice") committee (of which Cardinal George Pell was named president), founded by the Congregation for Divine Worship to oversee and regulate the English translation of liturgical texts. This committee and ICEL, along with those responsible for translations into other languages, were to follow the prescriptions of *Liturgiam Authenticam*, a document issued on March 28, 2001, by the Congregation for Divine Worship that changed the rules for translating the original Latin texts.

Now, in Francis, we have a truly Vatican II pope. In the first major document of his pontificate, *Evangelii Gaudium* (The Joy of the Gospel, November 24, 2013), he stressed the need for a sound decentralization. Accordingly, the Vatican's usurpation of the local bishops' work through ICEL, its legitimate commission, has come under the scrutiny it deserves.

This book will compare and contrast the 1998 and 2010 Missals and put the case for recognizing the clear superiority of the 1998 translation.

The new commission set up by Pope Francis may not concern itself directly with the question of whether or not there should be another translation of the Roman Missal. It does not need to. Waiting in the wings is a translation, prepared by the original ICEL and approved by all the English-speaking bishops' conferences. Take it down from a Vatican shelf, dust it off, and make a few additions. Then Mass in the vernacular can become, as it should be, a powerful tool of evangelization when people experience it.

My warm thanks to John Wilkins, editor of *The Tablet* for twenty-one years and a wonderful friend. He made available and updated a chapter for this book; he has also done an excellent job in checking and improving what I have written. Let me express my gratitude as well to John Batt, Paul Baumann (the editor of *Commonweal* who allowed me to reproduce John Wilkins's chapter), Philomena Billington, Bishop Paul Bird, Sean Burke, Brendan Byrne, Gilles Emery, Anne Hunt, Ruth McCurry, Brett O'Neill, Moira Peters, Roderick Strange, Christopher Willcock, and the librarians of the Dalton McCaughey Library. In different ways they all contributed to the making of this book. It is dedicated to Bishop Maurice Taylor, who served as chairman for the old ICEL's episcopal board and, in *It's the Eucharist, Thank God* (Brandon, Suffolk: Decani Books, 2009), told the story of ICEL's dismantling. Scripture quotations are usually taken from the New Revised Standard Version.

Gerald O'Collins, SJ
Jesuit Theological College
Parkville, Australia
Easter, 2017

Chapter One

The Missal That Never Was

by John Wilkins

*T*he reforming Second Vatican Council concluded its work in Rome in December 1965. The first document it promulgated was the Constitution on the Sacred Liturgy (*Sacrosanctum Concilium*). It was a trailblazer for what followed, harbinger of a new era for the church. The draft text lifted the spirits of one member of the council's central preparatory commission, the late Archbishop Denis Hurley of Durban, when he took it out of his briefcase during a journey from Rome to South Africa and started to read it.

He had been discouraged by the other material that he had seen; this was different. "For the first time," he testified, "I felt able to say: this council is going to mean something in the life of the church."

Archbishop Hurley, a prominent progressive at Vatican II who died in 2004 at the age of eighty-eight, was to play an important part in the International Commission on English in the Liturgy (ICEL), set up by bishops of the English-speaking world to translate into the vernacular the Latin liturgical books as reformed by the council and postconciliar commissions. It is a disturbing story. As editor from 1982 to 2003 of the Catholic weekly *The Tablet* in London, I had a rule of thumb to apply to the stream of instructions coming out of the Roman Curia. If the curial congregations became concerned about an issue, it should always be assumed that they had good reason. But the methods they used and their answers could be wrong. This twin-track assessment fits the ICEL case all too well. The early translations were done under great pressure and they contained many inadequacies. When ICEL itself set out to remedy these, its work foundered on Vatican distrust.

The use of vernacular languages in the liturgy of the Roman Rite did not begin with the Second Vatican Council. For decades previously, an array of Catholic scholars and experts had been doing research in France, Germany, the Low Countries, Italy, England, and the United States; centers of liturgical renewal had become influential; and by the early 1950s, Rome had commissioned conferences of bishops—already it was they who had the responsibility—to prepare translations of part of the rites for baptisms, marriages, and funerals. Precisely because so much preparation had been done, the bishops assembled for the council felt able to push ahead immediately with liturgical reform.

Few realized in those early days just how far the logic of the liturgical changes would take them. Repeatedly the council's Constitution on the Sacred Liturgy stressed that what the church desired was "full, conscious, and active participation in liturgical celebrations" by "all the faithful." This aim was "to be considered before all else"; here was "the primary and indispensable source from which the faithful are to derive the true Christian spirit." Full participation was "their right and obligation by reason of their baptism"; it was this that showed them to be "a chosen race, a royal priesthood, a holy nation, a redeemed people" (SC 14).

On December 4, 1963, at the end of the council's second session, the constitution was passed by a massive majority: there were only four dissenting votes. Archbishop Marcel Lefebvre, who would later lead a schismatic movement against the council's work, is said to have been in favor of it.

The overwhelming consensus was achieved in part because the opening to the vernacular was endorsed in guarded terms. "The use of the Latin language . . . is to be preserved in the Latin rites," the document cautioned, before opening up the way ahead: "But since the use of the vernacular, whether in the Mass, the administration of the sacraments, or in other parts of the liturgy, may frequently be of great advantage to the people, a wider use may be made of it." This passage was followed immediately by the commissioning of bishops' conferences to put the council's wishes into practice. It was the local bishops who had the responsibility "to decide whether, and to what extent, the vernacular language is to be used." Their decrees must then be confirmed by Rome, the document said (SC 36).

So from the first, local bishops were clearly understood to be in control of the liturgical translations. This approach was in line with one of Vatican II's key achievements, confirmed by a vote of the whole council on October 30, 1963. On that day, by a huge majority, the bishops affirmed that the church must be seen to be governed on the model of Peter and the Twelve. Leadership therefore belongs to the whole college of bishops, with and under the pope. Each bishop is a vicar of Christ in his own diocese (*Lumen Gentium*, Dogmatic Constitution on the Church, 27). Sharing of authority, within Catholic unity, is proper to the church. As with the liturgy, though, this necessary counterbalance to Vatican I's emphasis on papal and Roman power was a reform easier to approve in principle than to implement in practice.

Before the liturgy constitution was promulgated, the English-speaking bishops, who were the first to see the advantages of pooling their resources, had established the core of ICEL. In a formal meeting at the English College in Rome on October 17, 1963, ten English-speaking conferences agreed to share the translation work: those of Australia, Canada, England and Wales, India, Ireland, New Zealand, Pakistan, Scotland, South Africa, and the United States. By the time the council ended in 1965, the ICEL secretariat had been opened in Washington, DC. In 1967 the Philippines became the eleventh ICEL member; there were also fifteen associated conferences of countries that used English in the liturgy without its being the predominant language. A vast task awaited them: the translation of several thousand texts in some thirty distinct liturgical books. And that "full, conscious, and active participation" desired by the council would turn out to be a far more complicated undertaking than anyone had envisaged.

It quickly became evident that, once begun, vernacular translations had to go the whole way. The bishops were as eager as the priests and people. The Vatican Congregation for Rites, as it was then called (in 1969 it became the Congregation for Divine Worship), hesitated and made attempts at retreat, but in 1967 Paul VI gave the bishops' conferences his permission to press ahead.[1]

Those early years were frenetic. In Rome, the Vatican *consilium* for implementing the Constitution on the Liturgy, set up in 1964, worked night and day to complete *editiones typicae* in Latin and make them available to local bishops' conferences. The first Eucharistic Prayer was joined by three more in 1968. Sunday Mass sheets appeared each week. Liturgists burned the midnight oil as they debated how best to achieve a style appropriate to English usage. How to deal with the long periodic sentences that give the Latin its characteristic rhythm? ICEL decided to break them down into shorter components.

That preference triggered a battle royal. The aim was to achieve a noble simplicity of language that was true to the original while pleasing to the ear and apt for proclamation. But to what extent did simplification in the interests of modern sensibilities mean falsification? The more rhetorical style of the Latin presents a balance between God's action and the human response. Fierce criticism of the 1973 Missal accused it of trivializing the profundities of the original and of exalting human religious striving at the expense of the initiative of God, which is always prior.[2]

The ICEL texts were widely circulated for comment and critique. There was an attempt to enlist Catholic poets and writers, but they were not willing to participate: this was not, they felt, an assignment for them.[3]

---

[1] See Paul VI, "Concession," in ICEL, *Documents on the Liturgy 1963–1979* (Collegeville, MN: Liturgical Press, 1982), 278–79.

[2] This error has been traditionally called "Pelagianism," after Pelagius (active around 400), who taught that human beings can achieve salvation through their own sustained efforts. In "What Kind of Missal Are We Getting?" *New Black-friars* 77, no. 910 (1996): 548–52, Bruce Harbert wrongly detected Pelagianism in several collects found in the 1998 Missal (which he called ICEL 2). Ironically, given Harbert's role in preparing the 2010 Missal, Pelagianism clearly turns up in that translation.

[3] Unlike ICEL, those who prepared the 1966 Jerusalem Bible had succeeded in enlisting the help of such notable authors as J. R. R. Tolkien.

Considering the pressures, it is remarkable that so much was achieved. Nevertheless, when the first texts came out, the bishops of England and Wales were less than happy, and in the early 1970s they went ahead with their own version of the breviary; they were joined in this effort by the Scots, Irish, and Australians. They also issued their own partial translation of the Missal and of the funeral and confirmation rites, which turned out to be short-lived.

Two members of the International Theological Commission were also unhappy. One was Joseph Ratzinger, later to be head of the Congregation for the Doctrine of the Faith for twenty-three years and then John Paul II's successor as pope; the other was Chilean Jorge Medina Estévez, later cardinal and head of the Congregation for Divine Worship and the Discipline of the Sacraments, as it was renamed in 1975 after a merger (here CDW). In 2005, Medina would announce the name of the new pope, Benedict XVI, to the waiting world. Both had been among the signatories of a letter to Paul VI in 1972 complaining that the English, French, German, and Spanish vernacular translations were watering down and endangering the church's doctrine.[4] Paul VI listened but the Holy See's instruction to translators issued in 1969, a series of guidelines known by its original French title, *Comme le prévoit*, remained in force. But the two future leaders never forgot.

By 1978, ICEL had produced English translations of all the texts issued by Rome. The first versions had been published in a cheaper, provisional format for experimental use. Next, as had always been envisaged, came the time for revision. Everyone concerned with the

---

[4] Kevin Seasoltz provides a fuller account of this letter: "On October 11, 1972, [the future] Cardinal Medina and [the future] Cardinal Ratzinger and six other members of the International Theological Commission wrote to Pope Paul VI to express their urgent concern that the unity and purity of the Catholic faith were being severely compromised by inaccurate and theologically suspect translations of liturgical texts from Latin into the vernacular languages. They complained that the Congregation for Divine Worship was unwisely relying on local bishops' conferences to judge the quality of translated texts rather than examining them carefully in Rome," introduction to Peter Jeffery, *Translating Tradition: A Chant Historian Reads* Liturgiam Authenticam (Collegeville, MN: Liturgical Press, 2005), 7.

translations recognized the need for improvement. ICEL began this stage in 1982, aiming at a fuller, richer, more poetic and exalted tone. Behind the scenes, intense discussion continued about how best to achieve faithful translations that would enable English-speaking congregations to feel they were really praying in the living language—as requested by Paul VI.

ICEL was now at a zenith. There was time and space in the early 1980s to revise, amend, and refine, and the commission was proud of what it was producing. The Rite of Christian Initiation of Adults was taken out of storage and made available to the whole church. Before embarking on the mammoth task of revising the entire 1973 Missal, ICEL had decided to begin with the Order of Christian Funerals, a comparatively manageable project. In accordance with the mandate given by bishops' conferences in 1964 and by the Vatican in 1969 that the commission's work should extend to the provision of original texts, ICEL included some forty new prayers for situations not covered in the Roman books, such as suicides and the deaths of children. This was creative pastoral work. The reform was beginning to settle down and take root.

But the climate in Rome was changing. In 1978, Karol Wojtyla was elected pope, and he saw it as part of his mission to reimpose theological order and central control. In line with perceptions that a "restoration" was underway, John Paul II consulted all the bishops about allowing the former Tridentine rite to be more widely celebrated again. Almost the entire episcopate of the world opposed the proposal, on the ground that two forms of the Roman or Latin Rite within the one church would bring disunity. This had been the concern of Paul VI when he ruled in 1969 that the Tridentine Rite must be regarded as having been replaced.[5] He was acutely aware that for the

---

[5] An instruction of October 20, 1969, from the Sacred Congregation for Divine Worship approved by Paul VI admitted an exception in the case of "elderly priests who celebrate Mass without a congregation and who might encounter serious difficulty in taking up the new Order of Mass." They were allowed "with the permission of their Ordinary" to celebrate the Tridentine Mass. Further "special cases of priests who are infirm, ill, or otherwise disabled" were to be submitted to the congregation (*Documents on the Liturgy*, 537).

Lefebvrist dissidents, the Rite was a badge of rebellion against the Second Vatican Council—for them, he said, it was like the white flag of the French monarchists with its fleurs-de-lis.[6]

John Paul II went ahead regardless. In 1984 he issued an indult permitting the Tridentine Rite to be publicly celebrated in certain circumstances. Just as the bishops had feared, groups hostile to the Second Vatican Council's reforms took heart from the decision. The tide bearing ICEL along had now passed its peak, though at the time this was not apparent. Seeing the way things were going, bishops became more nervous. There was controversy over the question of inclusive language, which ICEL was already grappling with in the late 1970s.

Attention focused on the translation of the Psalter, which the ICEL board of bishops had wanted ever since the commission was founded. Because of the volume of work in the early years, it was not possible to begin this huge effort until 1979. Samples of the texts were sent out for comment in the 1980s, as the work moved forward. It would take fifteen years to complete the project.

Any commission charged with English translations at that time would have felt the need to use inclusive language. By the 1980s it was hardly possible in ordinary speech or writing to continue to use the words "men" or "man" as applying also to women. The ICEL translators felt their way forward, both on the horizontal level, where masculine collective nouns, pronouns, and adjectives described groups including both women and men, and on the vertical level, where references to God were wholly masculine. Women religious, concerned that they should not yet again be marginalized by terms that excluded them, lobbied powerfully and effectively.

ICEL adopted the stylistic norms approved by the US bishops' conference for the use of inclusive language in translating biblical passages. Some of the early texts attempt to reflect the complexity of the biblical material: "Lord God, your care for us surpasses even a

---

[6] See Sacred Congregation for Divine Worship, Notification June 1971, in *Documents on the Liturgy*, 544–46, at 545; Paul VI, address to a consistory May 24, 1976, in *Documents on the Liturgy*, 176–80, at 178; Paul VI, Letter to Archbishop Marcel Lefebvre October 11, 1976, in *Documents on the Liturgy*, 182–89, at 186.

mother's tender love." The critics made their alarm vociferously clear. ICEL had been taken over by the feminists, they announced, and had become an inclusive-language factory. There are masculine words in the Psalter that have always been taken in Christian tradition to presage the coming of Jesus Christ, "the Man." If those were changed, a theological dimension of the meaning of the text would be lost. Such objections were partial and exaggerated and, to an extent, discredited by inept translations that the objectors put forward as alternatives; nevertheless, some of the American bishops began to listen, and so did Rome.

ICEL's major work, the revision of the Roman Missal, began in 1982. In 1988, the first of three extensive progress reports was issued, to be followed, suddenly and unexpectedly, by the appearance of a threatening cloud on ICEL's horizon. The prefect of the CDW was now the German cardinal Paul Augustin Mayer, OSB, a brilliant linguist who had previously been secretary of the Congregation for Religious. There he had reined in American women religious who, in his view, had gone too far in rewriting their constitutions in accordance with the instructions of Vatican II. At one gathering, Mayer observed that the bishops approved some original prayers for the Missal simply "because they were on the market." The episcopal vote, he alleged, had become a rubber stamp. A religious sister who was present raised her hand. "Your Eminence," she asked, "do I understand you to say that the bishops haven't really prepared beforehand how to vote on these texts?" Mayer slammed his fist on the table. "I said nothing of the kind!" But he had. And in 1988, just before he stepped down at the age of seventy-seven, Mayer sent a letter to the conferences of bishops saying that ICEL needed to be reformed, restructured, and redirected.

The English-speaking bishops stood by their commission. In November 1988, ICEL's chairman, Archbishop Hurley, arranged for a meeting with Mayer's successor, Cardinal Eduardo Martínez Somalo. A former diplomat, Martínez was pleasant to deal with. The Mayer letter was put on the shelf and a few cautionary words were spoken, but for the time being harmony continued under Martínez and his successor, Cardinal Antonio María Javierre Ortas, prefect from 1992 to 1996. It was the calm before the storm.

Meanwhile, Pope John Paul II was exerting his iron will over the church. The ace in Rome's hand was the ability to appoint almost all the bishops in the world. In this way national conference after national conference was deliberately shunted toward the conservative side. The tendency was to choose "safe" men. As the effects of the policy took hold in the United States, some bishops of the American conference, which had formerly been so supportive of ICEL, began to take their distance.

They tuned in to a growing sense of alarm that many Catholics no longer had a strong sense of the Real Presence of Christ in the Eucharist. Surveys in the United States seemed to back this up, and the younger conservative American bishops began to point the finger at ICEL for allegedly underplaying the sense of the sacred. ICEL's more colloquial tone, they argued, was making congregations less respectful.

The revised Missal with its much heightened style had been cir-culated in 1992 to the bishops' conferences that owned ICEL. At their own request, the bishops were voting on it in eight segments, to avoid a repeat of 1973, when they had been hit with two thousand pages at once. Most conferences accepted the revision by overwhelming ma-jorities. Among the American bishops, though, there were some thirty who judged the translation of the Order of the Mass not sufficiently literal. When the American conference met in Chicago in 1995, this group was determined to reject the text. It was a tense, contentious discussion. The revised Missal needed a two-thirds majority to pass; it scraped by with only seven votes to spare. Rome noticed.

Next to run into trouble was the interim translation of the Psalter, published in 1995, with its use of inclusive language. It was never voted on, but the bishops released it for study and experiment. It was widely adopted, especially for use in Morning and Evening Prayer, by men and women religious and numbers of laypeople. In 1997, however, Cardinal Ratzinger requested that the *imprimatur* given by Baltimore's Cardinal William Keeler, president of the US conference, should be withdrawn, and it was.

The clouds were now dark across the sky. In June 1998, the storm broke. ICEL's episcopal board was holding its annual meeting in

Washington. They were anticipating the arrival of Cardinal Francis George, archbishop of Chicago, who was now the American representative on the board. Cardinal George was coming from Rome.

There was as usual a full agenda. The bishops had finished Morning Prayer and had just started their discussions when George arrived. As soon as the then-ICEL chairman, Bishop Maurice Taylor of Galloway, Scotland, had finished welcoming him, George asked that the order of the agenda be changed. He wanted immediate discussion of the relations between ICEL and the Vatican congregation. The bishops froze.

Bishop Taylor brokered a compromise. The agenda should be adhered to, he said, but provision would be made for the cardinal to address the meeting toward the end of the day. When the time came for Cardinal George to speak, in the late afternoon, he warned the participants that the commission was in danger. They were at a turning point. The principles that had governed ICEL's approach to translation had been rethought. Rome wanted a vernacular, he said, that was different from the vernacular of the contemporary marketplace, so as to lead worshipers into the nuances and deepest meanings of the texts.[7]

The project as ICEL understood it was no longer considered legitimate. According to George, the commission's thoroughgoing use of inclusive language in its translation of the Psalter had been one of the reasons for disillusionment among the American bishops. There was a pent-up impatience with the commission. If ICEL gave the impression that it owned the Second Vatican Council or the liturgy, it would make bad matters worse, he said. It had to change both its attitude and, in some cases, its personnel. Otherwise it was finished. If necessary, the American bishops would strike out on their own. George spoke vehemently.

Next morning, Archbishop Hurley made a frank and formal response, speaking from a script that he had written out in longhand. The ICEL board was grateful for the message, said Hurley, but disturbed by it. It appeared from what the cardinal had said that a fun-

---

[7] See the next chapter for this desire to have a "sacred vernacular," a principle embodied in *Liturgiam Authenticam.*

damental change had occurred in the attitude of the Congregation for Divine Worship toward translation theory. Instead of conveying an equivalence of *meaning* between the Latin and English texts, as had been ICEL's practice hitherto, the congregation now wanted translations that conveyed an equivalence of *individual words*.

The archbishop pointed out that he had himself participated in the debate at Vatican II over collegiality—the sharing of all bishops in the governance of the church. But the change in translation practice announced by the cardinal, and the manner in which he had expressed himself, seemed to Hurley to mark a distressing departure from the spirit of collegiality in favor of authoritative imposition. For about a dozen years, ICEL had been revising the 1973 Missal in accordance with the principles previously laid down. All this might now end in frustration and waste.

As for inclusive language, Hurley agreed that the Catholic tradition must be upheld, and certain words must not be subjected to unreasonable demands in the interests of inclusivity. But the concerns reflected in the use of inclusive language had come to stay. Good sense, faith, and trust in God would lead to a solution. Could not the cardinal convey to the CDW and the pope that the commission believed in fraternal dialogue as the best way of resolving differences?

In a further intervention, Cardinal George reacted strongly to Hurley. He felt he had been insulted, he said. He apologized if anyone had felt attacked by him, but he was telling the members of ICEL things they needed to hear. They must be receptive to criticism of their texts, but they were not listening. That was the road to disaster. It seemed to George that he would have to report to the American bishops that they must choose between ICEL and Rome. Several times he pushed back his chair, causing some of the participants to fear that he would walk out.[8]

In hearing George's rebuke, ICEL's episcopal board was doubtless also hearing Cardinal Medina Estévez, now head of the CDW. Some twenty-six years earlier, along with Joseph Ratzinger, Medina had been

---

[8] For letters from Cardinal George and John Wilkins about the June 1998 meeting, see *Commonweal*, January 27, 2006, 4, 26–27.

one of the signatories of the letter of complaint sent to Pope Paul VI. The bishops had already had a taste of what to expect. The year prior to George's bombshell, the CDW had for the first time denied its approval to an ICEL text, the interim revised ordination rite, which had been sitting on desks in the Vatican for several years. The letter of rejection to bishops' conferences that had approved the text and submitted it to Rome came with a list of 114 criticisms. These, it was later emphasized, were by no means exhaustive.

After the Vatican's objections, ICEL put all its energies into a complete revision of the ordination rite, which was ready to be sent to the bishops' conferences by 1999. Again there was opposition from a minority of American bishops whose numbers were growing. The group was led by Archbishop Justin Rigali of St. Louis (now retired). Bishop Taylor's attempted compromise misfired, and in October he received a severe reprimand from Cardinal Medina warning him that ICEL was completely off course.

Bishop Taylor asked for a formal meeting with the Vatican congregation, but Medina told him this would be premature until steps were taken to ensure it would be "wholly productive." Meanwhile, Medina continued, the congregation had noted irregularities in the preparation of the ordination rite. "For a number of years" the congregation had had to warn ICEL of "an undue autonomy" evident in the translations. But all such interventions, he contended, had met with "a lack of response." As a result, the CDW's task of "ensuring that translations accurately and fully convey the content of the original texts" had often been "hampered and delayed." Medina then accused the commission of paraphrasing and redrafting, and (contradicting the mandate given to ICEL by the bishops' conferences when it was set up, and subsequently confirmed by Rome) he declared that the CDW did not accept that the commission had the right to produce original texts.

There was more, much more, in this vein, leading to Medina's sweeping conclusion that "in its present form" ICEL was "not in a position to render to the bishops, to the Holy See, and to the English-speaking faithful an adequate level of service." The situation was of "particular gravity" considering "the prominence of the

English language in the international community." (The cardinal did not himself speak English.)

Then came a demand that amounted to nothing less than a takeover bid. Medina ordered that ICEL's "statutes" be "revised thoroughly and without delay" under the supervision of the CDW.

But ICEL did not have statutes. It had a constitution, precisely because it had been created by the bishops and was owned by them, not by the Vatican. As such, according to canon law, it did not need a status approved by Rome.

Aware that a fundamental principle—the governance given the bishops by Vatican II—was now at stake, Maurice Taylor as chairman of ICEL sought in every way to fend off this demand while mollifying the congregation. In an exchange of letters, he continued to speak of revising ICEL's "constitution." But Cardinal Medina was relentless. He spoke of "statutes" and he was going to get them.

In additional letters, the cardinal insisted that ICEL meet another new demand. Staff, experts, and translators working for the commission must receive clearance from Rome, he ordered, and all staff and experts used by ICEL so far must be replaced so as "to ensure a genuinely fresh start." He even threatened to deny the commission any further recognition. Meanwhile, the cardinal's second in command, Archbishop Francesco Pio Tamburrino, accused the ICEL bishops' conferences of subverting the Christian faith of their tens of millions of people.

A plea by Bishop Taylor to Cardinal Medina on July 12, 2000, shows a lamb among wolves. The cardinal's letter, the bishop noted, had spoken of "a grave crisis" that the Vatican congregation would have to resolve. Courteously, the bishop took issue: "To speak of a grave crisis seems to overlook the scope for dialogue in the present situation. The revised draft was composed exclusively by bishops (members of the episcopal board of ICEL) who represent various bishops' conferences and have their confidence. Is it not possible for a reasonable dialogue to take place between them and the congregation?"

Bishop Taylor went on to press the Vatican II principle of the governance of the church by the whole college of bishops: "The bishops are men of integrity and responsibility with wide pastoral experience who, presumably, also have the confidence of the Holy Father and the Holy See. If collegiality among bishops means anything, surely we may be allowed to explain our work to bishop-members (and other officials) of the congregation, to answer questions or concerns, and generally to be treated maturely in a matter all of us know to be of great pastoral importance for millions of Catholics in many countries."

But the CDW was moving toward its knockout blow. On March 28, 2001, it published a new instruction on the use of the vernacular, titled *Liturgiam Authenticam* (Authentic Liturgy), which overturned the entire basis on which ICEL's work had rested for nearly forty years. And in July a supervisory committee of cardinals and bishops known as *Vox Clara* (Clear Voice) was established to ensure that the Vatican would get exactly what it wanted. The English-speaking language group is the only one to have had such a committee imposed on it. *Liturgiam Authenticam* did not recommend; it commanded. It insisted that translations follow an extreme literalism, extending even to syntax and rhythm, punctuation, and capital letters. The clear implication was that in this way it would be possible to achieve a sort of "timeless" English above the change of fashion, a claim reminiscent of that made for the Ronald Knox translation of the Bible, which today is so dated that it is not read except as a period piece.

A stipulation that appeared to mark a further retreat from Vatican II perspectives ruled out ecumenical cooperation over liturgical translations. This meant the end of pioneering links begun in 1967 between ICEL and the North American Consultation on Common Texts and the International Consultation on English Texts (ICET). Moreover, according to *Liturgiam Authenticam*, "great caution is to be taken to avoid a wording or style that the Catholic faithful would confuse with the manner of speech of non-Catholic ecclesial communities or other religions, so that such a factor will not cause them confusion or discomfort."

Could the framers of the Vatican instruction really be suggesting that translations of the *Gloria* and Creed agreed upon with other churches were causing "confusion" and "discomfort" to Catholic parishioners who had heard them used in non-Catholic liturgies? As recently as 1995, in his ecumenical encyclical *Ut Unum Sint*, Pope John Paul himself had encouraged the preparation of agreed-upon texts for the prayers of the liturgy that the Christian churches have in common.[9]

When he first heard the news of *Liturgiam Authenticam*'s prescriptions, one American Presbyterian who for thirty-five years had worked to foster liturgical dialogue with the Catholic Church was so distressed that he slumped into a chair and wept. "I realized," wrote Professor Horace Allen, Emeritus Professor of Worship at Boston University, "that something terrible had happened which in my own worst imaginings I had never anticipated. A trusted and beloved ecumenical partner had suddenly and effectively walked away from the table."

Just when other churches were revising their liturgical books to match the common texts, the Catholic Church repudiated them. At future ecumenical services of the Word, congregations would no longer be able to pray the Creed and *Gloria* together, using the same words and knowing them by heart.[10]

A slashing critique of *Liturgiam Authenticam* appeared in four articles in 2004 in *Worship*, the American journal of liturgical renewal published by the monks of Saint John's Abbey, Collegeville, Minnesota. The writer was Peter Jeffery, Scheide Professor of Music History at Princeton University and an oblate of a Benedictine abbey, whose judgment was significant as it came from a conservative academic—in his own words, "as conservative as one can get without rejecting Vatican II." He too, he testified, "would like to see translations more

---

[9] John Paul II had done that indirectly, inasmuch as he recommended "ecumenical translations of the Bible" (*Ut Unum Sint*, 44) and, warmly and at length, encouraged "common prayer" among Christians (*Ut Unum Sint*, 22–26), even if he never explicitly spoke of "common texts" for that common prayer. He recalled numerous occasions on which he himself had prayed together with other Christian leaders (*Ut Unum Sint*, 24–25, 76), and, in particular, a meeting with the Ecumenical Patriarch Dimitrios I, "when we recited together the Nicene-Constantinopolitan Creed according to its original Greek text" (*Ut Unum Sint*, 24). That meant that John Paul II recited the Creed not only without the (later) Western addition about the Holy Spirit also proceeding from the Son (the "Filioque") but also starting with the "we believe" of the original Greek text—and not with the "I believe" that was to be imposed by the 2010 Missal.

[10] See Tom Heneghan, "At Loss for Words," *Commonweal*, November 18, 2005, 11–12.

literal than some of the ones we use now." He was at one with the authors of *Liturgiam Authenticam* in desiring "a more profound sense of the sacred." Still, their instruction struck him as "the most ignorant statement on liturgy ever issued by a modern Vatican congregation." It should be "summarily withdrawn," he argued, to allow time for "proper consultation with a sufficient number of experts."[11] (Incredible to say, those who wrote *Liturgiam Authenticam* never consulted ICEL as such, despite the commission's offer of its services.)

Drawing on his own wide understanding and on exhaustive research, Jeffery described the authentic tradition of the Latin Church and the Roman Rite as "a huge garden," filled with every sort of tree and flower and weed. By contrast, he wrote, the authors of *Liturgiam Authenticam* perceived the treasure of the liturgy as "fully excavated, catalogued, and safely stored in the Vatican museum."[12]

The truth was otherwise, declared Jeffery. The Catholic Church was still on its way: it had not arrived at its destination—all Catholics could at least agree on that. Let there be a clear view of the true task of liturgical renewal today. It was "an unprecedented effort." The challenge was "to develop a worship for a new world, in which near-universal access to scholarship has made most people capable of taking a more active role than was ever possible before in the history of the church."

In October 2001 the presidents of the ICEL bishops' conferences at last met with Cardinal Medina in Rome. He stomped all over them, like a schoolmaster confronting unruly pupils. They came out fuming impotently. As demanded by Medina, the staff and experts who had served the commission were dismissed, including the executive secretary, John Page, a layman who had particularly incurred Medina's ire. For thirty years Page had served on the staff of ICEL. The courteous and gentle American sat at the table during his last meeting with the episcopal board, in Ottawa in 2002, with tears streaming down his face.

---

[11] See Jeffery, *Translating Tradition*, 17, 23, 98, 100–101; this book gathered together the four articles originally published in *Worship*.

[12] Ibid., 54–55.

A year later, Medina retired from the CDW. One of his last official acts—symbolically—was to ordain priests in the Tridentine Rite, as though it were on an equal level in the church with the reformed rite. He was succeeded by Cardinal Francis Arinze. The Nigerian was affable and diplomatic, the soft cop to Medina's tough cop. The ICEL bishops had a day-long meeting with Arinze in October 2003, marking a significant moment in the history of John Paul II's papacy. By then they could fight no more. It was the final act of the drama, and everyone knew it. The bishops sued for peace. They surrendered the prerogatives granted them by their predecessors at the Second Vatican Council. It was now no longer they who created and maintained ICEL, but Rome. *Liturgiam Authenticam* even claimed Rome's right to impose its own translation.

The test of the new policies enforced by *Liturgiam Authenticam* would be the next translation of the English-language Mass. A draft appeared on an Australian website in 2004 and was published in the May 22 *Tablet* that year. It brought a flood of correspondence from the magazine's readers. They wanted to know why there had been no consultation. Was this translation really what then-Cardinal Ratzinger had in mind when he called for a "reform of the liturgical reform"?

One letter had a different tone. It came from the new chairman of ICEL, Bishop Arthur Roche of Leeds. Like the new ICEL secretary Fr. (rapidly promoted to Msgr.) Bruce Harbert, Roche was an Englishman. (Harbert had been one of the most persistent critics of ICEL; the poacher had become the gamekeeper.) Bishop Roche's letter deplored *The Tablet*'s publication of the text. It infringed ICEL's copyright, he said, adding, without a hint of irony, that it showed "disregard for the processes of bishops' conferences."

This was yet another U-turn. For nearly forty years it had been ICEL's policy that its procedures should be transparent and its draft texts and proposals widely diffused, on the ground that the task it performed was a public service to the whole church.

Somewhere on a shelf in the Vatican lies the 1998 ICEL Missal, the fruit of thirteen years of work, denied Rome's approval. Although it was passed by all eleven bishops' conferences as the long-awaited revision of its 1973 precursor, it has never been seen by the English-speaking world at large. Its rendering of the Mass achieves a beautiful flow, and the abbreviations and paraphrases that so seriously marred the 1973 version have been addressed. The quality of what it contains can be gauged from the collects. These opening prayers had drawn vehement and damaging attack as the weakest element of the 1973 book. Among the completely redone translations, here is one for the Twenty-Seventh Sunday in Ordinary Time:

> Almighty and eternal God,
> whose bounty is greater than we deserve or desire,
> pour out upon us your abundant mercy;
> forgive the things that weigh upon our consciences,
> and enrich us with blessings
> for which our prayers dare not hope.

Together with the collects translated from the Latin are alternative prayers newly composed by ICEL. Here are two. The first is for Midnight Mass at Christmas:

> Good and gracious God,
> on this holy night you gave us your Son, the Lord of the universe, wrapped in swaddling clothes, the Savior of all, lying in a manger.
> On this holy night draw us into the mystery of your love.
> Join our voices with the heavenly host, that we may sing your glory on high.
> Give us a place among the shepherds,
> that we may find the one for whom we have waited,
> Jesus Christ, your Word made flesh,
> who lives and reigns with you in the unity of the Holy
> Spirit, in the splendour of eternal light, God for ever and ever.

The second is for Good Friday:

> From the throne of grace, O God of mercy, at the hour your Son gave himself to death, hear the devout prayer of your people.
> As he is lifted high upon the cross, draw into his exalted life all who are reborn in the blood and water flowing from his opened side.

These latter texts are so successful that in the opinion of some commentators they carried a new risk—that they would always be chosen over the Roman ones. How could it have been right to leave work of this quality moldering in a Vatican cupboard while a rival group without comparable liturgical expertise started all over again, as if to reinvent the wheel? If any justification was to be offered for causing so many people pain and harassment, the new texts in their final form would need to be good. They were not.

Chapter Two

Translation into the Vernacular: Two Guidelines

*S*t. Jerome (d. 420) performed a monumental service for Western Christians by translating the (Hebrew and Greek) Bible into a contemporary vernacular: namely, Latin. Both liturgically and otherwise, his "Vulgate" translation enjoyed an enduring impact; the history of world Christianity has known no translator of biblical or other texts who was more significant. He was deeply aware of the challenges facing any translator, and he wrote: "If I translate word for word, it sounds absurd. If I am forced to change something in the word order or in the style, I will seem to have stopped being a translator."[1] Notice how Jerome did not say, "If I am forced to change something in the word order or style, I will have [truly] stopped being a translator," but only "I will seem [to some others] to have stopped being a translator." Uninformed critics could, he knew, accuse him of "betraying" the original text when, to express the meaning, he had to move beyond a literal, word-for-word translation. Many centuries later, in a play on words, Italians would express this criticism by saying, *traduttore traditore* (the translator is a traitor).[2]

---

[1] Jerome, preface to *Eusebii Pamphili Chronicorum Liber Secundus*, PL 27, 223–24. In the original Latin of his preface, Jerome wrote: "si ad verbum interpretor, absurde resonat; si ob necessitatem aliquid in ordine vel in sermone mutavero, ab interpretis videbor officio recessisse."

[2] On translators being charged with treachery and infidelity, see Robert Wechsler, *Performing without a Stage: The Art of Literary Translation* (North Haven, CT: Catbird Press, 1998), 58–94. Some outstanding modern translations

An older contemporary whom Jerome admired for his keen intelligence, Evagrius of Antioch (d. after 382), translated from Greek into Latin a life of St. Antony of Egypt. In a letter to a friend that formed the preface for the translation, Evagrius wrote: "A word-for-word translation from one language into another conceals the meaning and strangles it, even as spreading couch grass [does to] a field of corn." Addressing the friend for whom he had made this translation, Evagrius claimed: "Whatever lack may be in the words, there is none in the meaning. Let others go hunting after letters and syllables; do you seek for the meaning."[3]

In a letter to Pope Urban IV that formed the prologue for *Contra Errores Graecorum*, Thomas Aquinas, the greatest medieval theologian, stated: "It is . . . the task of the good translator, when translating material dealing with the Catholic faith, to preserve the meaning but to adapt the mode of expression, so that it is in harmony with the idiom of the language into which he is translating." Anticipating modern theories about "dynamic" equivalence rather than "formal" or "literal" correspondence, Aquinas rejected a word-for-word in favor of a meaning-for-meaning translation: "When anything expressed in one language is translated merely word-for-word into another, it will be no surprise if perplexity concerning the meaning of the original sometimes occurs."[4]

In his 1866 *Letter to Pusey*, John Henry Newman includes a passage on Marian devotion and doctrine that contains quotations from Justin, Tertullian, and Irenaeus. With laconic insight, he adds in a footnote: "I have attempted to translate literally, without caring to write English."[5]

---

have faced such criticism: for example, Seamus Heaney, *Aeneid Book VI* (London: Faber & Faber, 2016); Clive James, *The Divine Comedy of Dante: A New Verse Translation* (New York: Liveright, 2013).

[3] *Vita Antonii Abbatis*, PL 73, 125–26; translation from Helen Waddell, *The Desert Fathers* (London: Constable, 1936), 4; translation corrected. I thank Sean Burke for this reference.

[4] http://dhspriory.org/thomas/ContraErrGraecorum.htm. I thank Fr. Gilles Emery, OP, for this reference.

[5] John Henry Newman, *A Letter to the Rev. E. B. Pusey* (London: Longmans & Green, 1866), 36n2.

What would Newman think of a version of liturgical texts that set out to translate word for word, without caring to write acceptable English?

In an English understatement, Ronald Knox (d. 1957), himself a notable, if controversial, translator, spoke of the accusation of "sitting too loose to the originals."[6] Yet he converged with Jerome, Evagrius, Aquinas, and Newman: if "literalness" is "accepted as our rule, dullness is the result."[7] The central challenge for translators, according to Knox, is to create a text that, while faithful to "the originals," should itself "have the freshness of an original product" and that can be read "with the same interest and enjoyment which the reading of the original would have afforded." "In the long run," he emphasized, "the meaning is what matters."[8] One could quote other authoritative voices from the past and present who agree with Knox. Sacrificing everything to "fidelity" will lead to texts that fail to be natural, fresh, and even intelligible. Translations must sound like original compositions in the receptor language.

George Steiner (b. 1929), a Cambridge University polymath, summed up the task of translation as producing a "faithful but autonomous restatement." He explained: "The translator closely reproduces the original, but composes a text that is natural to his own tongue, which can stand on its own."[9]

From Evagrius of Antioch to George Steiner, there is unanimity that a genuine translation must communicate well. This aim was completely ignored by Cardinal Jorge Medina Estévez, a Chilean who was moved up to Rome, in his decree to accompany the third, "typical" edition of the 1970 *Missale Romanum* issued in the year 2000.[10] The new vernacular versions of this Missal should be "faithfully and accurately" prepared, he insisted. Not a word was said about their being

---

[6] Ronald A. Knox, *On English Translation* (Oxford: Clarendon Press, 1957), 9.

[7] Ibid., 12.

[8] Ibid., 5, 17, 21.

[9] George Steiner, *After Babel: Aspects of Language and Translation* (Oxford: Oxford University Press, 1977), 253.

[10] This decree is found in the opening pages of all English editions of the 2010 Roman Missal.

intelligible and clear in a way that would encourage something central to Vatican II's Constitution on the Liturgy: the full and active participation in worship by all those present.

I have recalled briefly what six authorities have said about the art of translation (Jerome, Evagrius, Aquinas, Newman, Knox, and Steiner), to provide a minimal background for discussing two Roman documents aimed at guiding those who translate official liturgical texts: *Comme le prévoit* ("As is foreseen") of January 25, 1969,[11] which for nearly three decades provided guidelines for the original ICEL (and similar bodies translating those texts into languages other than English), and *Liturgiam Authenticam* of March 28, 2001, which Bishop Maurice Taylor has called "a new weapon to restrain and subjugate ICEL."[12] While the 1969 instruction appeared in French along with five other major receptor languages into which the Latin liturgical texts were being translated, the 2001 instruction was simply published in Latin.[13]

Comme le Prévoit

The instruction, known from the opening words of its French edition as *Comme le prévoit*, emerged from a conference on translation in Rome (November 9–13, 1965) that was attended by 249 representatives and experts already working on translations around the world. The meeting aimed to learn from the experience of translators and

---

[11] ICEL, *Documents on the Liturgy 1963–1979: Conciliar, Papal, and Curial Texts* (Collegeville, MN: Liturgical Press, 1982), 284–91. On *Comme le prévoit,* also known in English as "The 1969 Instruction on the Translation of Liturgical Texts," see Keith Pecklers and Gilbert Ostdiek, "The History of Vernaculars and Role of Translation," in Edward Foley, gen. ed., *A Commentary on the Order of Mass of the Roman Missal* (Collegeville, MN: Liturgical Press, 2011), 35–72, at 59–63.

[12] Maurice Taylor, *It's the Eucharist, Thank God* (Brandon, Suffolk, UK: Decani Books, 2009), 61.

[13] Latin text and English trans., *Liturgiam Authenticam: Fifth Instruction on the Vernacular Translation of the Roman Liturgy* (Washington, DC: United States Catholic Conference of Bishops, 2001); an English translation is also provided by Peter Jeffery, *Translating Tradition: A Chant Historian Reads Liturgiam Authenticam* (Collegeville, MN: Liturgical Press, 2005), 123–65.

develop common guidelines for them. Few of the speakers referred to contemporary theories of translation. But many contrasted, as did Jerome, two approaches now often characterized as "literal" or "formal" (word-for-word) correspondence as opposed to "dynamic" or "functional" (meaning-for-meaning) equivalence.

In the aftermath of this meeting, the official *Consilium* for implementing the liturgical reform (established by Paul VI on January 25, 1964) consulted the commissions of various language groups around the world and prepared an instruction on translation. Amendments from Pope Paul VI were incorporated into the final text of *Comme le prévoit*, which was issued on January 25, 1969, in six major languages—a "remarkable example of worldwide consultation and collegiality."[14] It identified issues and offered wise guidance. Let us see six examples of this.

First, *Comme le prévoit* (CLP) followed Vatican II's lead, as expressed in the Constitution on the Sacred Liturgy (SC 36.3) by prescribing that, "when a common language is spoken in several different countries, international commissions should be appointed by the conferences of bishops who speak the same language to make one text for all" (CLP 2). It was on this basis that ICEL, which had been established on October 17, 1963, continued to do its work.[15] *Comme le prévoit* showed no intention of interfering with the situation in which conferences of bishops appointed commissions like ICEL and those commissions reported to their respective episcopal conferences.

All that was changed in the late 1990s, when the Congregation for Divine Worship and the Discipline of the Sacraments peremptorily and unilaterally asserted its control over ICEL. It did so in a detailed manner. For instance, except for members of the Episcopal Board, everyone working for ICEL (read: liturgical experts) now had to receive clearance from the congregation.[16] What began as a commission serving conferences of English-speaking bishops was now subordinated to a Vatican congregation. Closing his account of this scandalous takeover, Bishop Taylor "wondered" how "the congregation, or indeed

---

[14] Pecklers and Ostdiek, "The History of Vernaculars," 60n86.

[15] See ibid., 61–63, and Taylor, *It's the Eucharist*, 38–41.

[16] See Taylor, *It's the Eucharist*, 47–70.

the Holy See itself, would have reacted if the conferences of bishops, or even the conference presidents, had claimed that their legitimate authority had been infringed by the congregation's behaviour."[17]

Second, *Comme le prévoit* set its face against word-for-word translations or even phrase-for-phrase translations. That could, in fact, "obscure or weaken the meaning of the whole." The instruction insisted that "the 'unit of meaning' is not the individual word but the whole passage" (CLP 12). Hence "a faithful translation . . . cannot be judged on the basis of individual words" (CLP 6). Rather, a genuine translation reproduces the original meaning; it provides meaning for meaning. Concerned more with meaning than with individual words, it refuses "to conceal and strangle the meaning" and declines to join others who "hunt after letters and syllables" (Evagrius) or translate "merely word for word" (Aquinas), or who "translate literally, without caring to write English" (Newman).

Third, *Comme le prévoit* expected translators to keep in mind "the literary form proper" to the receptor language (CLP 6). This recalls Jerome's attention to that language's "style," Aquinas's respect for "the idiom" of the receptor language, Newman's "care to write English," Knox's desire to find a translation presenting itself with "the freshness of an original product," and Steiner's call for "a text that is natural to" the translator's own tongue and "can stand on its own." The instruction offered some examples of how Latin style may not correspond to that of other languages. In Latin, "the piling up of *ratam, rationabilem, acceptabilem* may increase the sense of invocation."[18] But in other languages, "a succession of adjectives may actually weaken the force of the prayer. . . . The same is true of . . . the too casual use of superlatives." What is natural to the Latin language may not be natural to other languages; as an example the instruction mentioned English and its habit of "understatement" (CLP 12).

---

[17] Ibid., 70.

[18] These three Latin adjectives are found in the Eucharistic Prayer of the pre–Vatican II Missal within a cluster of five adjectives that belong to the final blessing before the consecration: "Quam oblationem tu, Deus, in omnibus, quaesumus *benedictam, adscriptam, ratam, rationabilem, acceptabilemque* facere digneris: ut nobis Corpus et Sanguis fiat dilectissimi Filii tui Domini nostri Iesu Christi."

Fourth, "adaptation," "change," and even "paraphrasing" may sometimes be necessary (CLP 21, 23, 33). *Comme le prévoit* mentioned, in particular, the Opening Prayer, Prayer over the Gifts, Prayer after Communion, and Prayer over the People. Coming "from the ancient Roman tradition," they can be "succinct and abstract" and "may need to be rendered somewhat more freely while conserving the original ideas. This can be done by moderately amplifying them or, if necessary, paraphrasing expressions" (CLP 34). We will see later in detail how brilliantly this was done for the 1998 Missal "that never was." Those who do not have access to the text of this Missal can, at any rate, consult *Opening Prayers*, its proposed opening prayers published by Canterbury Press (Norwich) in 1999.

Fifth, over and over again *Comme le prévoit* emphasized the need for translations of liturgical texts to communicate well and facilitate participation (CLP 6, 8, 14, 20, 41).[19] They should prove easily intelligible when proclaimed, sound natural rather than awkwardly foreign, and promote prayer. Thus the instruction directed that "translations must be faithful to the art of communication in all its various aspects" (CLP 7). The "intelligibility of prayers when said aloud" may at times have to take "precedence" over "verbal fidelity" (CLP 29).

With an eye on those who share in the liturgy, *Comme le prévoit* insisted: "The language chosen should be that in 'common usage,' that is, suited to the greater number of the faithful who speak it in everyday use, even 'children and persons of small education. . . .' No special literary training should be required of the people" (quoting from an allocution of Paul VI). In short, "liturgical texts should normally be intelligible to all, even to the less educated" (CLP 15). This guideline, which emerges naturally from Vatican II's Constitution on the Sacred Liturgy, has clearly shaped the choice of intelligible English throughout the 1998 Missal that the Vatican refused to confirm. By way of contrast, as we will see in chapter 3, the English of the 2010 Missal remains too often impenetrable to "ordinary" people; it can sound like Latin texts trans-

---

[19] Here the instruction showed its full fidelity to what Vatican II's Constitution on the Liturgy mandated: "full, conscious, and active participation in liturgical celebration" (SC 14).

literated into English words and masquerading as English. A classic example comes with the choice of "consubstantial" in the Nicene Creed. Sixth, picking up the teaching from the Constitution on the Sacred Liturgy, *Comme le prévoit* observed that, for a "fully renewed liturgy," the "creation of new texts will be necessary" (CLP 43). Note that the instruction calls the composition of original texts not merely licit but necessary. The original ICEL did just that, by composing, for instance, brilliant opening prayers that echo the gospel passages to be read in a given liturgical year (see chapter 5 below).

Before moving to *Liturgiam Authenticam*, it is worth adding that *Comme le prévoit* speaks of historical matters accurately. It recalled, for instance, that in the Latin liturgy "many of the phrases of approach to the Almighty were originally adapted from forms of address to the sovereign in the courts of Byzantium and Rome." Hence translators should "study how far an attempt should be made to offer equivalents in modern English for such words as *quaesumus, dignare, clementissime, maiestas*, and the like" (CLP 13). Unfortunately, those who prepared the 2010 Missal, as we will see below, seem to have failed to put this question to themselves.

Liturgiam Authenticam

Admittedly, here and there *Liturgiam Authenticam* stated that translators should produce texts that can be easily understood so as to facilitate the participation of all those assembled for worship (LA 20, 21, 25, 27, and 28). But even these articles heavily qualified such intelligibility with provisos. Article 20, for instance, mandated an exact translation, free of omissions, additions, paraphrases, and glosses. What the instruction called translating "most accurately [*accuratissime*]" (LA 55) constituted a turn toward word-for-word translation, an approach often called "literal or formal correspondence." By contrast, *Comme le prévoit* advocated a meaning-for-meaning approach, often called "dynamic equivalence," even though this 1969 document never uses that term.

Liturgiam Authenticam prescribed retaining from the Latin source as much as possible of the syntax (for example, the relative and subordinate clauses), vocabulary, and even capitalization. The instruction wanted a "sacred style" (*stylum sacrum*), which could differ from current speech and even sound strange and "obsolete" (LA 27, 43). It dreamed of a "sacred language" (*lingua sacra*) with its own "vocabulary, syntax, and grammar," which might have its impact on "daily speech" (LA 47). Where current English and other languages have turned toward "inclusive" speech, the "sacred language" should not follow suit. The gendered language of Latin was not to be altered (LA 30–31).

Liturgiam Authenticam occasioned many reactions and reviews, both negative and positive.[20] The most authoritative and careful critique has come from a chant historian of Princeton University who places himself on the conservative side of the Roman Catholic spectrum, Professor Peter Jeffery. His four articles, originally published in *Worship* for 2004, were put together a year later in a book, *Translating Tradition: A Chant Historian Reads* Liturgiam Authenticam. He finds the people who wrote the instruction to be "seriously misinformed about the historical development of the tradition they call on us to preserve." *Liturgiam Authenticam* is simply "full of misstatements about the Roman liturgical tradition."[21]

Let me take two painful cases of such historical misinformation. First, the instruction speaks of a sacred vernacular created in the past by the Roman Rite (LA 47; see also 59). Jeffery asks: "When and where did liturgical translation of the Roman rite create a sacral vernacular that even shaped everyday speech?" He shows that "what historical documents reveal is quite unlike *LA*'s picture of liturgical language moulding vernacular speech."[22] Out of ignorance, the authors of *Liturgiam Authenticam* simply rewrote history for their own purposes.

Second, the instruction asserts that in the Creed "we believe" violates "the tradition of the Latin Church." But, as Jeffery points out, it is "simply untrue" to claim that "not only the Roman rite, but the broader Latin Church as a whole shares a uniform tradition in favour of 'I believe,' as if 'we believe' were essentially an Eastern tradition."

---

[20] See Pecklers and Ostdiek, "The History of Vernaculars," 66.

[21] Jeffery, *Translating Tradition*, 17; see chap. 1 above for what John Wilkins drew from Jeffery's criticism.

[22] Ibid., 66, 67; for the historical evidence that he produces, see ibid., 65–76.

"The original texts of the so-called Nicene Creed . . . began 'we believe,' as reported in numerous Latin and Greek sources." Jeffery gives examples: "the plural 'we' form was cited by Pope Leo the Great, and in early Roman collections of canon law." For good measure, Jeffery adds that the Mozarabic Rite of Spain "has always said 'we believe,' both before and after Vatican II. Even in the Roman Mass there was a minority tradition that used 'Credimus' instead of 'Credo.'"[23]

He presses on to illustrate how other "inaccuracies, misrepresentations, and contradictions abound" in *Liturgiam Authenticam*; he tackles what it asserts about capitalization, the Kyrie, and the *Trisagion* of Good Friday.[24] We noted above how the instruction, in the name of being true to the patrimony of the Roman Rite, outlaws omissions, additions, paraphrases, and glosses. Jeffery shows how, on the contrary, the Roman Rite "did not insist on integral and exact textual renditions, while it did make use of omissions, additions, paraphrases, and glosses."[25] He piles up the evidence to conclude that *Liturgiam Authenticam* "is remarkably uninformed about the history of the Roman and Latin liturgical traditions."[26]

Jeffery shows deep concern that "what it [*Liturgiam Authenticam*] lacks in factuality it makes up with naked aggression. It speaks words of power and control rather than cooperation and consultation, much less charity." He argues that *Liturgiam Authenticam* is "the most ignorant statement on liturgy ever issued by a modern Vatican congregation," and "should be summarily withdrawn."[27]

We have looked at some details of Jeffery's evaluation of *Liturgiam Authenticam*. Other scholars widely criticized the Vatican instruction for requiring translators to practice verbal equality with the original Latin, and to follow its grammar and syntax. Such strict adherence to the Latin original ignored the fact that English—to cite the vernacular we are concerned with—does not have a Latin structure in its

---

[23] Ibid., 18–19.
[24] Ibid., 22, 23–29.
[25] Ibid., 39.
[26] Ibid., 52.
[27] Ibid., 97, 98, 100.

sentences. Contemporary English does not indulge, for instance, the long sentences of Ciceronian and classical liturgical Latin. The guidelines from *Liturgiam Authenticam* would not produce a recognizably English vernacular but Latin texts transposed into English words, texts that regularly sound more Latin than English.

There should be no need to pursue matters further. *Liturgiam Authenticam* is seriously deficient in its guidelines for translating liturgical texts. Unlike the immeasurably superior *Comme le prévoit*, it could never claim to stand in the tradition of the wise instructions from Evagrius of Antioch, Jerome, Aquinas, and others who encourage a meaning-for-meaning rather than a word-for-word translation. To bolster its case for opening the Creed with "I believe" (*Credo*) rather than "we believe" (*Credimus*), *Liturgiam Authenticam* takes one look back before the Council of Trent and cites Aquinas. But, as Jeffery demonstrates, the instruction simply misinterprets Aquinas.[28] Naturally it never attends to the rule for translators found in Aquinas's letter to Urban IV, nor does it attend to ancient Christian sources quoted by Jeffery.

Thus far *Liturgiam Authenticam* has not been withdrawn.[29] In the years following its publication in 2001, it became the book of rules for the new ICEL and the *Vox Clara* committee, who produced the translation for the 2010 Missal. It was also meant to guide the new vernacular translations (into other languages) of all missals that Cardinal Medina Estévez required to be prepared in the aftermath of the third edition of the *Missale Romanum* in 2002, a minor revision of the 1970 original. "The preceding versions in use until now," he instructed in a preface to that *Missale Romanum*, were all to be "emended accurately in fidelity to the original Latin text."[30] At the start of this chapter we remarked on his emphasis on translations being "faithful" and "accu-

---

[28] Ibid., 18–21.

[29] Just before Christmas 2016, however, Pope Francis established a commission, headed by Archbishop Arthur Roche and to include bishops from all continents, that is to revisit *Liturgiam Authenticam*. For the outcome, see postscript below, 114.

[30] Letter of April 20, 2000; reproduced in the opening pages of all editions of the 2010 Missal.

rate," without anything being said about their being intelligible and clear. This alleged "fidelity," inculcated by *Liturgiam Authenticam*, normally would not go below the surface level of the Latin (source) language to seek out the basic meaning expressed by the text, and would be content with a literal, formal "transference" into the receptor languages, the various vernaculars.

In doing their work, the members of the new ICEL and *Vox Clara*, unlike the original ICEL,[31] did not share their work with a wider public. They worked in strict confidentiality (read: lack of transparency), even if *Vox Clara* regularly published sanitized reports of their activity.[32] Let us turn now to the English-language Missal they produced in 2010.

[31] See Taylor, *It's the Eucharist*, 43–45.
[32] See Pecklers and Ostdiek. "The History of Vernaculars," 67–68.

Chapter Three

The Roman Missal of December 2010

*W*riting in 2005 and 2009, respectively, John Wilkins (chapter 1) and Bishop Maurice Taylor provided vivid accounts of how the drama that affected the translation of the Roman Missal into English unfolded.[1] But how would it finally play itself out?

In February 2006 the new ICEL and *Vox Clara* issued the final draft of their translation, the so-called "gray book." The eleven English-speaking bishops' conferences approved the "gray book" and also proposed some changes toward a revised version accepted by the Vatican in June 2008. A final *recognitio*, given on March 26, 2010, was announced a month later at a meeting of *Vox Clara* with Pope Benedict XVI on April 28, 2010. But when, on August 20, 2010, the English translation of the Order of Mass was made public, it contained over one hundred changes to the text of 2008 that had received the official *recognitio* in March 2010. Even more dramatic news came on December 31, 2010, when the text of the Roman Missal was sent to seven publishers for preparation and release. Around ten thousand changes had been made in the "gray book" revised and approved by the bishops' conferences. Astonishingly, even *after* securing the reluctant agreement of English-speaking bishops to their new translation, the Congregation for Divine Worship, through *Vox Clara* and the new ICEL, unilaterally introduced thousands of changes, some

---

[1] Maurice Taylor, *It's the Eucharist, Thank God* (Brandon, Suffolk, UK: Decani Books, 2009).

of which were of a relatively minor nature (such as punctuation) but some of a substantial nature. It was this text that was imposed on English-speaking Catholics from the First Sunday of Advent 2011.[2]

The 2010 Roman Missal had been prepared under the auspices of Cardinal George Pell as president of *Vox Clara*, Archbishop Arthur Roche as chairman of the new ICEL (2002–2012), and Monsignor Bruce Harbert as executive director of the secretariat of the new ICEL (2002–2009). They and their colleagues worked, of course, according to the guidelines of *Liturgiam Authenticam*, but added their own touches. Let us see, for instance, how those guidelines were unpacked in several principles that Harbert has endorsed for translating the Latin liturgy into English.

Some Principles from Harbert

In a brief review for *New Blackfriars*,[3] Monsignor Harbert proposed as one principle for translation that "the *effect* of a text on its original audience should be reproduced" (emphasis original). This ignores the fact that, as with much of the Latin liturgy, we have no idea whatsoever who constituted, for example, "the original audience" of the Roman Canon, let alone the effect on them of the text that they were hearing for the first time. We need to recall that it "was composed of a number of distinct prayers over the course of several centuries."[4] Who then would be the "original audience"? Those, whoever they were, who heard the text that John Baldovin quotes from Ambrose of Milan? Those who heard the Roman Canon as it became more or less stable in the sixth century? We should label Harbert's principle "the original audience fallacy."

It resembles "the intentional fallacy" (that is to say, the original author fallacy) of Eric Donald Hirsch (b. 1928), professor emeritus of

---

[2] See Edward Foley, gen. ed., *A Commentary on the Order of Mass of The Roman Missal* (Collegeville, MN: Liturgical Press, 2011), xvii–xxviii.

[3] *New Blackfriars* 95 (2014), 625–26.

[4] On the historical emergence of the Roman Canon, see John Baldovin, a leading American liturgist, "History of the Latin Text and Rite," in Foley, *A Commentary on the Order of Mass*, 247–53, at 250.

the University of Virginia.[5] He argued for the theory, now discredited by many philosophers, literary critics, experts in jurisprudence, and biblical exegetes, that texts mean *only* what their authors intended to communicate. In Hirsch's view, texts function as a bridge between the minds of the authors and those of subsequent readers. The latter have the role of grasping and restating now what the authors consciously wished to convey then. Harbert's "original audience fallacy" understands traditional liturgical texts to function as a similar bridge—between the minds and emotions of the original audience and those who perform these texts today. Translators of such texts, he holds, should aim at allowing contemporary worshipers to grasp for themselves and reproduce the impact these texts had on the worshipers who first experienced them.

In the same review, Harbert remarks that a central principle for the 2010 translation was "a sacral style that will inspire its users." Here he uses an old-fashioned adjective by speaking of a "sacral style" rather than a "sacred style," as *Liturgiam Authenticam* did (see previous chapter). Such a "sacral style" and, for that matter, a "sacred style" seem alien to the model of all Christian prayers, the Our Father. Such a style simply does not characterize petitions like "thy will be done," "give us this day our daily bread," and "deliver us from evil." Jesus never suggested that we would honor God more and find ourselves more "inspired" by adopting a "sacral style" in our prayers, as if we should say: "may thy will, we pray, be graciously done"; "graciously grant us today our daily bread"; or "grant, we pray, that we may be mercifully delivered from evil."

Furthermore, it is the straightforward and not particularly "sacral" style of the psalms that fed Jesus' own prayer and made them enduringly effective as prayers for Jews and Christians alike. Their language is simple and powerfully direct and does not keep intelligibility at bay: "Have mercy on me, Lord. I have no strength"; "I will praise you, Lord, with all my heart"; "Lord God, I take refuge in you." A sacral style was not the style that inspired either Jesus or the psalmists. Did Harbert

[5] E. D. Hirsch, *Validity in Interpretation* (New Haven, CT: Yale University Press, 1967).

and his associates set up a human "tradition" and fail to follow the example and teaching of Jesus himself?

Some remarks of St. Cyprian of Carthage in his treatise *On the Lord's Prayer* seem apropos: "To pray otherwise than he [Jesus] taught us is more than a mistake, it is a fault, for he laid down: 'You reject the commandment of God in order to set up your own tradition.' Let us pray as our Master himself taught us. Our prayer is friendly and intimate when we petition God with his own prayer" (chapters 2 and 3). Surely the teaching and example of Jesus should be the supreme rule not only for Christian life but also for Christian liturgy? Would Harbert and his colleagues answer this question with an unqualified yes? One of them, Cuthbert Johnson, has quoted Thomas Aquinas on the Lord's Prayer as "the most perfect of prayers."[6]

Harbert remarks correctly on the vivid contrast "between the Scriptural style [of Jesus and others] and the Roman [read: Latin] one." He goes on to say rightly that "Roman rhetoric does not translate easily into modern English, nor are modern English speakers readily receptive to ancient Roman culture." But this was no excuse for what the translators of the 2010 Missal chose: "a path that lies midway between" the "lofty" and "elaborate style" of ancient Latin of the ancient Roman Canon and "a modern English style."[7] The result has been the "halfway" translation that often is no longer Latin but not yet acceptable modern English. I wonder how Jerome, John Henry Newman, and the other authorities quoted at the beginning of chapter 2 would judge this unabashed plea for a third style, neither ancient Latin nor modern English. Harbert and his coworkers followed the odd directives of *Liturgiam Authenticam*, which, as we noted in the last chapter, prescribed a special, "sacred style" that could differ from current speech and even sound strange and "obsolete" (LA 27, 43).

Finally, in his review Monsignor Harbert echoes *Liturgiam Authenticam* (LA 72) when he insists that "it is a mistake to entrust the liturgy

---

[6] Cuthbert Johnson, *Understanding the Roman Missal* (London: Catholic Truth Society, 2011), 78.

[7] Bruce Harbert, *Companion to the Order of Mass: The New Translation* (London: Catholic Truth Society, 2011), 88.

to a few powerful hands." But one might well ask: was it a mistake to seize control of the translation of the liturgy into English and put it into the hands of the few powerful people who made up the *Vox Clara* committee and the new ICEL that the Vatican carefully controlled? Was it a mistake to abandon the old ICEL's practice of transparency and to act for the most part in secrecy? Was it a mistake to introduce unilaterally thousands of changes into translations already approved by the English-speaking bishops' conferences?

Other Criticisms

Some supporters of the 2010 translation have appealed to the fact that around the world those who were to prepare translations into other languages often knew English but had at best a limited knowledge of Latin (in which the *Missale Romanum* appeared in 1970). They could turn to the English translation for guidance. This strange view pictured the English translation as a kind of "crib" for other translations and refused to acknowledge that an odd, Latinized translation fails to meet the liturgical needs of the native English-speakers and inhibits their sharing in worship. If translators for other language groups need a "crib" as they grapple with the original Latin, by all means let someone supply them with such an aid. But why foist on English-speakers what is hardly more than a "crib" of the original Latin text, the *Missale Romanum* of Paul VI with its minor revisions of 1975, 2002, and 2008?

Surveys in the United States, the British Isles, and New Zealand have shown how seriously dissatisfied the majority of laypeople and clergy are with the 2010 Missal.[8] Too often its new, "sacral" renderings are hard to proclaim, unpleasant to listen to, and difficult to understand. Following *Liturgiam Authenticam*, the translators forgot how Vatican II's Constitution on the Sacred Liturgy (and *Comme le prévoit*) insisted

---

[8] In "Why Pope Francis Is Right to Revisit the New Mass Translation" (*America*, for January 27, 2017), Michael G. Ryan cited a survey conducted by Georgetown University's Center for Applied Research in the Apostolate: only 27 percent of priests in the USA held that the 2010 translation lived up to expectations; more than half believed it urgently needed to be revised.

on a lucid clarity that would facilitate active sharing in public worship by all, even the less well educated. Michael G. Ryan, pastor of St. James Cathedral in Seattle, has commented: "such slavish attention to the Latin" has resulted in "translations that are museum pieces—about as fresh as a fossil preserved in amber."[9] When I complained about the new translation to an English bishop, I was told: "Give it time. You will get used to it." "Yes," I replied, "it will be like getting used to a colleague in the office who speaks bad English. I may be obediently resigned to this translation, but I could never approve of it or welcome it." Perhaps I should have quoted the late Peter Steele, a leading poet and master of the English language: "This new translation sounds like something written by people for whom English was a second language."

So far we have been looking more at headlines than at small print. Let me now move to eight areas in which the deficiencies of the new translation show up: the choice of odd, "stately" words; obsequious ways of addressing God; the failure to use inclusive language; inaccurate rendering of the Nicene Creed, which is in fact the Nicene-Constantinopolitan Creed of 381; a total lack of ecumenical sensibility; misleading or even mistaken translations; and theological language that could lead people seriously astray. Here and there we will illustrate the deficiencies of the 2010 Missal by comparing it with the 1998 Missal that the Vatican summarily dismissed.

Eight Areas of Failure

First, a desire for more formal, even "sacral" language dictated the repeated preference in the 2010 translation for "charity" over "love," "compunction" over "repentance," "conciliation" over "reconciliation," "fount" over "fountain," "laud" over "praise," "participate" over "share," "regeneration" over "being born again," "replenished" over "nourished," "solace" over "consolation," "supplication" over "prayer," "sustenance" over "food," and "wondrous" over "wonderful."[10] Speaking of an

---

[9] Michael G. Ryan, "Mission Intelligible," *The Tablet*, November 29, 2014, 12.

[10] Such "sacral" language belongs to the "pseudo-sacred," distinguished by its "remote air of pomp and circumstance": Josef Pieper, *In Search of the Sacred*:

"oblation" rather than an "offering" or "sacrifice" can leave hearers wondering whether the priest has stumbled over the word "ablution." "Oblation" no longer has currency in contemporary English.[11] In the Creed "consubstantial" (straight from the Latin *consubstantialis*) has replaced the user-friendly translation "of one being."[12] We return to this below. The 2010 Missal clearly favors old-fashioned English words that hardly belong to the spoken and written English of today. Did the translators believe that such old-fashioned language, which they may have claimed to be "timeless English," was the appropriate language in which to address God? Presumably they would have "defended" themselves by saying that they were following the instructions of *Liturgiam Authenticam* to use a "sacred language" that differed from current speech and could sound strange and even "obsolete" (LA 27, 43, 47).

"Prevenient grace" belongs to a theological treatise rather than to a liturgical translation. But there it is in the prayer over the offerings that *Vox Clara* included in the 2010 Missal for the feast of the Immaculate Conception:

> Graciously accept the saving sacrifice which we offer you, O Lord, on the Solemnity of the Immaculate Conception of the Blessed Virgin Mary, and grant that, as we profess her, on account of your prevenient grace, to be untouched by any stain of sin, so through her intercession, we may be delivered from all our faults.

Contributions to an Answer, trans. Lothar Krauth (San Francisco: St Ignatius Press, 1991), 21.

[11] Harbert recognizes this: "oblation" is "not common in ordinary English speech." He pleads in excuse: oblation "has been used on several occasions to avoid the monotony that would arise from overuse of 'sacrifice' and its more familiar synonyms [e.g., offering]" (*Companion to the Order of Mass: The New Translation* [London: Catholic Truth Society, 2011], 57).

[12] Cuthbert Johnson defends the use of "consubstantial" by arguing that "the Church has her own theological vocabulary which cannot be discarded" (*Understanding the Roman Missal*, 36). Discarding "consubstantial" is not the issue; it has its place in history as the term used in traditional Latin translations of the (Greek) creed from the Council of Constantinople of 381 (not 385, as Johnson states: ibid., 34). The issue is, rather, which translation of the original *homoousios* is more intelligible for a Sunday liturgy in the contemporary English-speaking world: "consubstantial" or "of one being" or "of one nature"?

Set this single, Latinized sentence, which belongs to Ciceronian and classical liturgical Latin, over against what the 1998 Missal proposed:

> In your goodness, Lord, receive the sacrifice of salvation which we offer on the feast of the immaculate conception. We profess in faith that your grace preserved the Virgin Mary from every stain of sin; through her intercession deliver us from all our faults.

There is no competition. "Your grace preserved" catches the meaning of "prevenient grace," and this 1998 translation—with its two sentences and the second one broken by a semicolon—follows the rhythm of spoken English. The 2010 translation, on the contrary, seems to have disassembled the long Latin sentence, substituted English words on a one-to-one basis, capitalized three words that were in lower case in the Latin text (*solemnitate, immaculatae,* and *beatae*), and then reassembled the lot in a jerky, breathless whole.[13]

Second, Jesus told us to address God in a childlike, straightforward fashion. In the last chapter we saw how the 1969 instruction *Comme le prévoit* questioned whether translators should seek equivalents for "the phrases of approach to the Almighty" that the Latin liturgy "adapted from forms of address to the sovereign in the courts of Byzantium and Rome" (CLP 13). The 2010 Missal relentlessly pursues, however, the unctuous or fulsome path of those courts, with "graciously" incessantly introducing prayers: "graciously grant," "graciously accept," "graciously choose," and so forth. "We pray" is likewise regularly inserted. It is not enough to say, "Look, Lord, on the offerings we make."

---

[13] In one long sentence, the Latin original reads: "Salutarem hostiam, quam in solemnitate immaculatae Conceptionis beatae Virginis Mariae tibi, Domine, offerimus, suscipe dignanter, et praesta, ut, sicut illam tua gratia praeveniente ab omni labe profitemur immune, ita, eius intercessione, a culpis omnibus liberemur." By introducing capital letters *even* when the Latin uses the lower case, the translators presumably aimed at enhancing a "sacral" effect. They regularly capitalize nouns referring to Christ (e.g., cross, resurrection, and kingdom). "The overall effect," the late Anscar Chupungco, a Filipino liturgist, commented, is only "distracting" ("EP RI: The ICEL2010 Translation," in Foley, *A Commentary on the Order of Mass,* 477). See Tom Elich, an Australian liturgist, "The ICEL2010 Translation," in Foley, ibid., 331–32.

This must become "Look, we pray, O Lord, on the offerings we make." It is not enough to say, "May your sacraments, Lord, perfect in us what lies within them." This must become "May your sacraments, O Lord, we pray, perfect in us what lies within them." (Both examples are taken from the Thirtieth Sunday in Ordinary Time.) Persistently, even though the celebrant is obviously engaged in prayer to God, "grant" must be lengthened to "grant, we pray." Such redundancy is not good English. Nor does it correspond to what Jesus said about being simple in prayer and not multiplying unnecessarily what we say (Matt 6:7-8).

In the 2010 Missal, addressing the divine persons becomes too often a formal affair that assumes an inappropriate "you who" shape. See, for example, the opening words of the prayer said by the celebrant of the Eucharist after the Our Father: "Lord Jesus Christ, who said to your Apostles." If I had been speaking to Barack Obama, I might have begun: "Mr. President, you said last year . . ." It would have sounded very odd to have said: "Mr. President, who said last year . . ."

Over and over again the translation of the opening prayers in the 2010 translation takes the "you who" form. The season of Lent abounds in such "you who" addresses to God: for example, the collects on the Monday, Thursday, and Saturday of the Second Week, and on the Fourth Sunday of Lent.

Such opening prayers can require a deep breath from the celebrant when they form one long sentence. Take the collect for the Epiphany: "O *God, who* on this day revealed your Only Begotten Son to the nations by the guidance of a star, grant in your mercy that *we, who* know you already by faith, may be brought to behold the beauty of your sublime glory" (emphasis added).[14] The 1998 translation, as far as I can see, never opens prayers with the "O God, who" form of address. It renders the Epiphany opening prayer, for instance: "God of mystery, on this day you revealed your only Son to the nations by the guidance of a star. We know you now by faith; lead us into that presence where we shall behold your glory face to face." This translation avoids the

---

[14] As Ronald Knox rightly observed, "there is no reason to use long sentences in your translation, because your author (Cicero, for example) uses long sentences" (*On English Translation* [Oxford: Clarendon Press, 1957], 21).

clumsy "we who" that turns up here and elsewhere in the 2010 translation. It is also much easier to proclaim—with two sentences and the second broken by a semicolon—and avoids the roundabout "grant in your mercy that we may be brought" by proposing a simple "lead us" that parallels the language of Jesus himself.[15]

A third deficiency of the 2010 translation, noted by many, comes when it follows the instructions of *Liturgiam Authenticam* (LA 30–31) and refuses to use consistently inclusive language. On the one hand, translating the Latin *et in terra pax hominibus bonae voluntatis*, the second line of the *Gloria* says: "and on earth peace to people of good will." This respects the fact that the Latin *homines*, unlike *viri*, is not gender-specific. But, on the other hand, for the Nicene Creed the translation renders *propter nos homines* as "for us men." What about "for us women"? Here one could translate the Latin as "for us human beings," or "for us men and women." The 1998 translation implies this inclusive meaning by simply saying "for us."

The 2010 translation notoriously maintains gender-exclusive language in its rendering of the Fourth Eucharistic Prayer: "You formed man in your own image and entrusted the whole world to his care, so that in serving you alone, the Creator, he might have dominion over all creatures," and so forth. Apart from flouting the Genesis teaching about God creating "male and female" in the divine image, this translation could have avoided offense by rendering the Latin: "You formed us in your own image and entrusted the whole world to our care, so that in serving you alone, the Creator, we have dominion over all creatures." The 1998 Missal translates: "You formed man and woman in your own likeness and entrusted the whole world to their care, so that in serving you alone, their Creator, they might be stewards of all creation." "Stewards of all creation" is better English than "have dominion over all creatures," and a happier translation from a biblical and theological point of view.

---

[15] In the original Latin of the 1970 Missal, this opening prayer says: "Deus, qui hodierna die Unigenitum tuum gentibus stella duce revelasti, concede propitius, ut, qui iam te ex fide cognovimus, usque ad contemplandam speciem tuae celsitudinis perducamur."

Fourth, Catholics value the Nicene-Constantinopolitan Creed not only because it classically sums up their faith but also because they share it with all Christians. It is the official creed on which the World Council of Churches was founded in 1948. The original English (1973) translation of the 1970 Missal introduced several brilliant features in its rendering of the Creed. The 1998 translation followed suit.

(i) It went back to the original "we believe" (*Credimus*) in the Greek text of the First Council of Constantinople (381 AD), instead of retaining the frequent but not exclusive Latin *Credo* or "I believe" (see Peter Jeffery in the last chapter). "I believe" belongs to the Apostles' Creed. If we continue to speak of the Nicene Creed (or, more accurately, the Nicene-Constantinopolitan Creed), we should be true to the text of 381.

(ii) The traditional Latin translation *ex Patre natum ante omnia saecula* and *genitum, non factum* was also unfaithful to the original Greek, which used the same verb each time: "eternally begotten [*gennēthenta*] of the Father" and "begotten [*gennēthenta*], not made." The 1998 translation, like its 1973 predecessor, maintained the double use of "begotten." The 2010 translation, ignoring the Greek original, rendered the two phrases differently: "born of the Father before all ages" and "begotten, not made." This lost the parallelism that the original Greek expressed by twice using *gennēthenta*; it followed the Latin version by misleadingly translating in different ways the same participle that occurred twice within a few lines.

(iii) The 1973 English translation rendered as "of one Being with the Father" the Greek phrase *homoousion tō patri*, and the 1998 translation did the same. This renders the original Greek at least as accurately as did the traditional Latin *consubstantialem Patri*, and is more easily understood than the transliterated "consubstantial with the Father" of the 2010 Missal.

(iv) Unlike the 2010 translation and also unlike the 1973 translation, the 1998 version of the Nicene Creed was properly inclusive. It confessed the incarnation "for us and for our salvation," and avoided possible misconceptions by not referring to the Holy Spirit as "he": "We believe in the Holy Spirit, the Lord, the giver of life who proceeds from the Father and the Son, who with the Father and the Son is worshiped and glorified, who has spoken through the prophets."

(v) When translating such parts of Eucharist as the *Gloria*, the Creed, and the *Sanctus*, the 2010 translation, following the instructions of *Liturgiam Authenticam*, left behind any desire to continue using translations already shared in common with other Christians. The result is that Catholics who attend other Christian services can find themselves saying (or singing) what they, as Catholics, *used to say or sing.* The 2010 translation vividly lacked any ecumenical sensibility and the conviction that common forms of prayer could help the cause of Christian unity. Having shared for many years with other Christians some translations, the English-speaking Catholic Church was forced to drop these and move out of step with those whom Pope Francis calls "our fellow pilgrims."

Long before the 2010 Missal appeared, *Liturgiam Authenticam* had excluded ecumenical cooperation from the mandate given to *Vox Clara* and the new ICEL. For many Catholics (and other Christians) the saddest result of this decision was the failure to settle or preserve a common form of words when praying the Lord's Prayer, either in a eucharistic setting or beyond.[16]

(vi) Sometimes the translation offered by the 2010 Missal is misleading. Take, for example, the prayer after Communion for the Thirtieth Sunday in Ordinary Time. The Latin text of the *Missale Romanum* of 1970 runs: *perficiant in nobis, Domine, quaesumus, tua sacramenta quod continent, ut quae nunc specie gerimus, rerum veritate capiamus.* The 2010 translation of the Missal renders this: "May your Sacraments, O Lord, we pray, perfect in us what lies within them, that what we now celebrate in signs we may one day possess in truth." Here we may hear an unfortunate contrast between "now celebrating [in mere and even empty?] signs" with "one day possessing in truth." The 1998 translation gives proper weight to *specie* and says: "Lord, may your mysteries accomplish within us the salvation they embody, [so] that we may come to possess in truth what we celebrate now under sacramental signs." This gives appropriate sense to what *specie* means in the tradition as "sacramental signs." The translation

---

[16] See Elich, "The ICEL2010 Translation," in Foley, *A Commentary on the Order of Mass*, 607–9.

introduces "mysteries," an alternate translation for "sacraments," so as to avoid a jarring repetition: "sacraments" and then "sacramental signs."

At times the 2010 translation is simply mistaken. Take, for instance, the prayer after Communion for the First Sunday of Advent, which also turns up on the Monday and Thursday of the First, Second, and Third Week of Advent. The Latin text of the 1970 *Missale Romanum* prays: *prosint nobis, quaesumus, Domine, frequentata mysteria, quibus nos, inter praetereuntia ambulantes, iam nunc instituis amare celestia et inhaerere mansuris.* The 2010 Missal renders this: "May these mysteries, O Lord, in which we have participated, profit us, we pray, for even now, as we walk amid passing things, you teach us *by them* to love the things of heaven and hold fast to what endures" (emphasis added). English-speaking hearers (or readers) naturally refer "by them" to the "passing things," whereas the sense of the Latin is clear: we are taught by the "mysteries" and not by the "passing things." The 1998 translation avoids this mistake and expresses the prayer in elegant and attractive English: "Lord our God, grant that in our journey through this passing world we may learn from these mysteries to cherish even now the things of heaven and to cling to the treasures that never pass away." Here, as so often elsewhere, there is no competition between the two translations.

(vii) Despite the concern of *Liturgiam Authenticam* to be theologically sound (for example, LA 26), the translators of the 2010 Missal introduced language that could lead people astray. Let me cite four examples of this.

1. A proper sensitivity to St. Paul's teaching about justification coming through faith and not through works should have ruled out occurrences of "meriting" that seem to diverge from orthodox Christian faith and lapse into Pelagianism. Take the prayer after Communion for the eighth Common of the Blessed Virgin Mary in Ordinary Time: "Renewed by the Sacrament [once again an obsession with capitals!] of salvation, we humbly beseech you, Lord, that we, who have honored in veneration the memory of the Blessed Virgin Mary, Mother of God, may merit to experience in

perpetuity the fruits of your redemption."[17] Here as elsewhere, the Latin original uses a form of *mereo* or *mereor*. But respect for the fact that we do not earn eternal salvation should discourage translating the verb as "earn" or "merit" and encourage us to translate it as "be found worthy" or even "receive." As the greatest of the Latin fathers of the church, St. Augustine of North Africa, put it, "if, then, your good works are God's gifts, he does not crown your merits as your merits, but as his own gifts."[18] The first preface for feasts of saints expresses the same truth: "you are glorified in your saints, for their glory is the crowning of your gifts."

Bruce Harbert rightly objects to Pelagian implications creeping into liturgical translations.[19] But, over and over again the 2010 Missal deploys the language of "merit" in ways that suggest that we achieve salvation through our own efforts.

2. In the Apostles' Creed the 2010 translation replaces "descended to the dead" (*descendit ad inferos*) with "descended into hell."[20] Eastern icons show the difference: Christ has descended to save the just ones who are long dead and waiting for him in the realm of the dead, "the limbo of the ancestors" (*limbus patrum*). He is not consorting with Satan, the devils, and human beings condemned to hell, as if he were prefiguring Dante's visit to the Inferno. As Anscar Chupungco remarks, translating *inferos* as "hell" is "perplexing." It revives an old English translation that, however, "does not correspond to the current understanding of hell."[21]

3. As regards the Nicene-Constantinopolitan Creed, one mistake appears in both the 1998 translation and that of 2010. Accurate theology reserves *credo in*, followed by nouns in the accusative

---

[17] As two further examples among very many, see the Prayers over the People for Friday after Ash Wednesday and for the Friday of the Second Week of Lent.

[18] Augustine, *Answer to the Pelagians*, IV, *Grace and Free Choice*, 15, trans. Roland J. Teske (Hyde Park, NY: New City Press, 1999), 81.

[19] Bruce Harbert, "What Kind of Missal Are We Getting?" *New Blackfriars* 77 (1996), 548–52, at 551.

[20] In the Fourth Eucharistic Prayer the 2010 translation speaks appropriately, however, of Christ's "descent to the dead" (*descensum ad inferos*).

[21] Chupungco, "The ICEL2010 Translation," in Foley, *A Commentary on the Order of Mass*, 184.

case, to the profession of faith in the Trinity, as in the Creed: *credo in unum Deum; credo in unum Iesum Christum; credo in Spiritum Sanctum*. When the church is the object of *credo*, the preposition is not used. One says simply *credo Ecclesiam*, to "acknowledge the nature and authority of the church and accept its teaching."[22] Both the 1998 and the 2010 translation, however, misleadingly profess belief not only "in" one God, one Lord Jesus Christ, and the Holy Spirit, but also "in" the one church.

4. At the express direction of Pope Benedict, the 2010 translation replaced "for you and for all" with "for you and for many" in the words the priest says over the chalice at the consecration. What should we make of this switch from "all" to "many," or rather the reversal to "many" since "all" had been used in the liturgy for nearly forty years?

This was a change with which eucharistic liturgies in other languages were also threatened by Pope Benedict XVI. He resigned in 2013 before effecting such a worldwide change. As far as I know, apart from the latest Spanish translation for the church in Mexico, it has come only in the English-speaking liturgy. In the vernacular renderings of the Eucharistic Prayers either revised (the Roman Canon) or introduced (the other Eucharistic Prayers) after the Second Vatican Council, the German, Italian, Portuguese, and Spanish translations all spoke of Christ's death "for all" rather than "for many."

Where should we turn for help in translating and interpreting the words that Mark's gospel (followed by Matthew, but not found in Luke and Paul) reports Jesus to have said over the cup: "This is my blood of the covenant, which is poured out for many"? In a letter to the German Bishops' Conference (April 24, 2012) outlining his reasons for reverting to "for many," Pope Benedict drew attention to some relevant passages in the New Testament, as well as to a title for Jesus, "the new Adam." Let us see the details.

In his Letter to the Romans, Paul declares that it was "for all of us" that God allowed his Son to die (8:12). The apostle writes twice in another letter of Christ dying "for all" (2 Cor 5:14-15).

[22] Ibid., 183; see Peter Jeffery, *Translating Tradition: A Chant Historian Reads Liturgiam Authenticam* (Collegeville, MN: Liturgical Press, 2005), 20–21.

The classic New Testament passage contrasting Adam with Christ the new Adam comes in Romans 5:12-21. We can sum up Paul's argument this way. The disobedience of Adam had a universal, evil effect. Christ's obedience did much more than merely reverse the universal results of Adam's sin. When expressing the universal impact of Adam and Christ, the apostle (who writes in Greek) sometimes uses the term *pantes* or "all" (verses 12 [twice] and 18 [twice]) and sometimes *hoi polloi* or "the many" (verses 15 [twice] and 19 [twice]). Paul's usage makes it obvious that he takes the Greek terms to be equivalent. He understands "the many" to be "all" human beings. This is quite unlike the situation in English, where "many" or "the many" are clearly not synonymous with "all."

What led Paul to introduce "the many," instead of simply using "all" throughout that passage in Romans 5? Was it merely a matter of "elegant" variation? Another explanation is possible. The apostle might well have envisaged a traditional contrast between "the one and the many"—in this case between the one (obedient) Christ and the many (sinners), who are in fact all human beings.

Another text that Pope Benedict cited in his letter of April 2012 (but without drawing the appropriate conclusion) was 1 Timothy 2:6: Christ Jesus "gave himself as a ransom for all." Probably taken from an early Christian creed, this phrase understands the self-sacrificing love of Christ to benefit *pantes* or "all." A parallel statement in Mark's gospel says that "the Son of Man came to give his life for many" (*polloi*) (10:45). The two passages express the same meaning: Jesus gave himself or surrendered his life to set all human beings free from the slavery of sin. First Timothy corrects a misunderstanding into which unwary readers of Mark 10:45 might slip. It was "for all" that Christ gave his life and not merely "for the many."

But when we come to Mark 14:24 (which uses *polloi*), should we insist on translating "the blood of the covenant poured out for many" and then explain that this means "for all"? We face a Semitic mindset: the "many" includes all and excludes none. The meaning is inclusive (the sum total which consists of many, or—in other words—the whole world), but not exclusive (many, but not all). In short, the "many" of Mark's text includes all and excludes none. In English, it is misleading to insist on "many" when we know what is meant. "All" is meant.

Here one should add that liturgical texts have not purported to be exact translations, which insist on rendering word for word and ignoring meanings. The classic Latin liturgical texts echo, adapt, add to, and weave together biblical passages. Such texts are not offered as strict translations of the original Hebrew or Greek. They are primarily concerned with conveying meaning, as well as evoking appropriate emotions and shaping intentions and actions.

In the New Testament we find *four different versions of the words of eucharistic institution.*[23] The earliest turns up in 1 Corinthians 11:23-25, to which Luke 22:19-20 approximates, but not word for word. Then Mark 14:23-24 is followed, again not word for word, by Matthew 26:26-28. Obviously when celebrating the Lord's Supper, the early Christian communities allowed themselves some freedom in the words they attributed to Jesus. No attempt was made to settle precisely the words that he used (in Aramaic) on the night before he died, with the aim of imposing that version uniformly.

Those who centuries ago fashioned the Roman Rite wove together words and phrases from the New Testament sources. The words of eucharistic institution that we have inherited from them do not correspond precisely to any of the four original sources: Paul, Luke, Mark, and Matthew. Neither in the New Testament nor in later liturgical texts did fidelity to Jesus involve trying to establish the words he used and then rigidly following them. Peter Jeffery illustrates how the Roman Rite did not insist on "integral and exact textual renditions, while it did make use of omissions, additions, paraphrases and glosses."[24]

Take, for instance, the words prescribed in the English Missal from 1973 to 2011: "this is the cup of my blood, the blood of the new and everlasting covenant. It will be shed for you and for all, so that sins may be forgiven." All four New Testament sources speak of "my blood" and of "the covenant"; only Paul and Luke name this covenant as "new"; and none of them calls it "everlast-

---

[23] See Chupungco, "EP RI: The ICEL2010 Translation," in Foley, *A Commentary on the Order of Mass*, 478–81.

[24] Jeffery, *Translating Tradition*, 39; see the whole chapter "The Bible in the Roman Rite," 32–57.

ing." Mark and Matthew say that Christ's blood will be shed "for many" (= for all), and Luke says that it will be shed "for you." Paul simply has Christ saying, "this cup is the new covenant in my blood," without explicitly adding that this blood will be shed for anyone. The shedding of Christ's blood "for the forgiveness of sins" is found only in Matthew's version of the Last Supper.

The history of the celebration of the Eucharist yields two conclusions relevant to our enquiry. First, the New Testament shows that the early Christians enjoyed a flexible openness in using four differing versions of the words of institution. Second, our Roman Rite claimed its own freedom by blending together the four versions and adding a few words of its own, as happened when it called the new covenant "everlasting." Neither here nor elsewhere did the Roman Rite aim at providing a literalist translation of the words of the Bible. It has always been in the business of creatively communicating the profound meaning of what Jesus said and did for the salvation of all.

Fidelity to Jesus does not involve a woodenly literal translation. What it does call for, from priest and people, is sharing with all their hearts in that celebration and joining their hearts with Jesus—an active participation made easy when the text clearly states the meaning of what Jesus intended and did at the Last Supper. His words and actions showed that he was willing to shed his blood *for all people*.[25] Mark and then Matthew wrote in Greek about Christ's death "for many." In today's English this means that he died "for all."

The Second Vatican Council's Constitution on the Liturgy repeatedly endorsed the principle that the texts and their meanings should be easy to understand, and should not "normally require much explanation" (SC 34). After forty years of hearing that Christ laid down his life "for all," switching to dying "for many" unfortunately requires such explanation. Otherwise people could be misled into thinking that Christ did not die "for all." The reversal promoted by Pope Benedict to "for you and for many" can too easily suggest that Christ died for some but not for others.

[25] See Gerald O'Collins, *Christology: A Biblical, Historical, and Systematic Study of Jesus*, 2nd ed. (Oxford: Oxford University Press, 2009), 67–80.

In his letter to the German Bishops' Conference, the pope insisted that Jesus at the Last Supper showed that he understood
himself as the Suffering Servant of Isaiah 53. Beyond question,
early Christians thought of the crucified Jesus in those terms.
But it is by no means historically certain that Jesus understood
himself precisely in the light of Isaiah 53.[26] Benedict also alleged that an earlier scholarly agreement about Isaiah 53:11-12
and the "many" (for whom the servant suffers) meaning "all"
had "collapsed." It was news to the biblical scholars that their
consensus about the Hebrew idiom meaning "all" no longer ex-
isted. What had happened was that the pope no longer accepted
their consensus. Seemingly it was for that reason rather than in
the name of the *pro multis* of the 1970 Latin original (and its
predecessors), which he never mentioned in his letter, that Pope
Benedict wanted to change back to "for many." Whatever the
precise papal reasons, Anscar Chupungco considers that "in the
entire corpus of the ICEL2010 Order of Mass," reverting to "for
many" is probably the most regrettable example of a slavish
application of literal translation.[27]

Why Pope Benedict insisted on "for many" becomes more
puzzling when we read his *Jesus of Nazareth*, where he cited
Isaiah 53 and various New Testament texts and concluded: "If
Isaiah used the word 'many' to refer essentially to the totality of
Israel, then as the Church responds in faith to Jesus' new use of
the word, it becomes increasingly clear that he did in fact die for
all."[28] If so, why cannot we continue to say so at the Eucharist?

(viii) A final failure of the 2010 Missal is that it does not allow
easy proclamation. It persistently uses, as we have observed, long
sentences that are difficult to proclaim. Such syntax belongs to the
language of Cicero and early church Latin, but not to contemporary English. Furthermore, the 2010 translation every now and then

---

[26] Ibid., 78–79.
[27] Chupungco, "EP RI: The ICEL2010 Translation," in Foley, *A Commentary on the Order of Mass*, 481.
[28] Benedict XVI, *Jesus of Nazareth*, vol. 2, *Holy Week, From the Entrance into Jerusalem to the Resurrection*, trans. Philip J. Whitmore (San Francisco: Ignatius Press, 2011), 137–38.

produces expressions that prove to be clumsy and even tongue-twisters. Take, for instance, the institution narrative over the bread in all four Eucharistic Prayers to be used in "Masses for various needs." Without modifying them the 2010 Missal translates two temporal clauses: "on the day before he was to *suffer*, on the night of the Last *Supper*." Some, even many priests, stumble over the awkward alliteration, "suffer" and then "Supper." By translating the meaning of the text, the 1998 Missal came up with an elegant version that maintains the sense of the two temporal clauses and is much easier to proclaim: "On the eve of his passion and death, while at table with those he loved."[29]

Cuthbert Johnson, an advisor to the *Vox Clara* committee, has praised the 2010 Missal for its "dignity, beauty and doctrinal precision."[30] But he makes no claims about any use of contemporary English and the ease with which texts can be proclaimed (by the celebrant) and understood (by those who hear them). The kind of "doctrinal precision" achieved by terms like "consubstantial" and "prevenient grace" belongs to theological treatises, not to liturgical proclamation. Its choice of language, over and over again, stops this translation from communicating well and facilitating the participation of the assembled faithful. Moreover, as we have seen, the 2010 Missal contains too many passages that are doctrinally misleading and mistaken, even to the point of favoring a Pelagian tendency. As for the "dignity" and "beauty" that Johnson (in an act of self-praise?) finds in the 2010 translation, does he mean the dignity and beauty that might attach to archaic English? Very many priests, religious, and laypeople do not detect much dignity and beauty in the 2010 Missal; they experience it as clumsy, awkward, and even ugly.

There is much to criticize in the 2010 Missal produced by *Vox Clara* and the new ICEL. In making these criticisms, we occasionally compared this translation with the 1998 Missal and found the latter persistently superior. Let us now look directly and in greater detail at this text produced by the first ICEL in the light of the instruction *Comme le prévoit*.

---

[29] See Chupungco, "The ICEL2010 Translation," in Foley, *A Commentary on the Order of Mass*, 572.

[30] Johnson, *Understanding the Roman Missal*, 3.

Chapter Four

The Suppressed Translation of 1998

*S*amples from the 1998 Missal have already appeared in earlier chapters. This chapter and the next chapter will let that translation emerge fully from the shadows that have cloaked it. Those burdened by the unhappy 2010 Missal have a right to know what they lost through the actions of Cardinal Medina Estévez and his associates. This chapter will sample some features of the Order of Mass in "the Missal that never was." We begin by selecting four items from the Introductory Rites: the opening greeting; the people's response; the penitential act; and the *Gloria*.

Introductory Rites

(1) The 1998 Missal begins with three alternative *greetings*: "The grace of our Lord Jesus Christ, the love of God, and the fellowship of the Holy Spirit be with you all" (A); "The Lord be with you" (B); "The grace and peace of God our Father and the Lord Jesus Christ be with you" (C). The first greeting picks up the "trinitarian" benediction with which Paul closes his Second Letter to the Corinthians (2 Cor 13:13), while the third matches the benediction with which the apostle normally opens his letters (for example, 1 Cor 1:3; Phil 1:2). "The Lord be with you" (the second greeting) comes from the angel Gabriel's opening words to Mary (Luke 1:28) at the annunciation of Jesus's conception and birth.

The 2010 Missal also provides these three greetings, leaving (B) untouched and slightly modifying (C): "Grace to you and peace from

God our Father and the Lord Jesus Christ." The translation of (A) is changed: "The grace of our Lord Jesus Christ, and the love of God, and the communion of the Holy Spirit be with you all." By inserting the "and" after "Lord Jesus Christ," it makes the greeting slightly stilted. The greeting does not run as "trippingly on the tongue" (William Shakespeare, *Hamlet*) as does the version offered by the 1998 Missal. Moreover, "the communion of the Holy Spirit" replaces a robust word of English origin ("fellowship")[1] with one of Latin origin ("communion"). At the start of the Eucharist, which will climax with the Communion Rite, it seems a little confusing to speak of "the communion of the Holy Spirit." The Holy Spirit will be invoked (in the epiclesis) to come down and change the assembled faithful, who will receive the risen Christ in Holy Communion. Admittedly, the text of the 1970 Missal has *communicatio Sancti Spiritus*, and in Latin *communicatio* is roughly equivalent to *communio*. But both *communicatio* and *communio* can also be translated as "fellowship"—something encouraged by the Pauline origin of this greeting. The Greek *koinōnia* in 2 Corinthians 13:13 is normally translated "fellowship."[2]

(2) The 1998 Missal maintains the *answer from the people* introduced by the 1973 Missal: "and also with you." Here the translation (from the Latin *et cum spiritu tuo*) found in the 2010 Missal, "and with

---

[1] The liturgies of Anglicans and other Christians have long used "fellowship," especially in the formula taken from 2 Corinthians 13:13. The word also received fresh currency from J. R. R. Tolkien's *The Lord of the Rings,* one of the top-selling books of the twentieth century.

[2] The New American Bible, the New Jerusalem Bible, the Revised English Bible, and Revised Standard Version all translate *koinōnia* as "fellowship," while the New Revised Standard Version stands alone in having "communion." Bruce Harbert recognizes how this greeting is taken from the closing words of 2 Corinthians, uses the Revised Standard Version, but then changes its translation to "communion" (*Companion to the Order of Mass* [London: Catholic Truth Society, 2011], 6). Cuthbert Johnson writes: "it is possible that Saint Paul was quoting words of greeting which were already in current use in the first Christian communities" (*Understanding the Roman Missal* [London: Catholic Truth Society, 2011], 10). In Paul's 2 Corinthians, however, these are words of farewell, not of greeting; the majority of commentators understand the Apostle himself to have crafted this farewell.

your spirit," seems preferable. This answer, widely used in Greek and Latin liturgies, looks back to the farewell greeting to a community in 2 Timothy 4:22: "the Lord be with your spirit." It also evokes a text drawn from a homily attributed to Epiphanius of Salamis (d. 403)[3] and read in the Divine Office on Holy Saturday. When Adam caught sight of Christ who had descended to the *limbus patrum*, he cried out to everyone in that realm of the dead: "My Lord be with you all." Christ answered him: "and with your spirit." Neither in 2 Timothy nor in this ancient homily does "spirit" refer merely to the spiritual side of human existence; it encompasses the whole human being. "Spirit" represents, in Anscar Chupungco's words, "the highest and noblest level in a human being." That is the sense of Mary's cry of joy: "my spirit rejoices in God my Savior" (Luke 1:47). Chupungco recognizes how a "modern holistic view of the human person" may have influenced the 1973 Missal (followed by the 1998 Missal) into offering the translation "and also with you." But this "fails to convey the full sense of the original formula."[4] Significantly, the translations in French, German, Italian, and other modern languages render *et cum spiritu tuo* as "and with your spirit."[5]

(3) The opening greeting and response in the 2010 translation are followed by the penitential act, introduced by the presiding priest: "Brothers and sisters, let us acknowledge our sins, and so prepare ourselves to celebrate the sacred mysteries." Here the 2010 Missal rightly corrects the 1973 Missal's weak translation of *agnoscamus* as "let us call to mind our sins." But it retains a false translation given by the same 1973 Missal ("prepare ourselves to celebrate the sacred mysteries"). Anscar Chupungco points out that "prepare ourselves" is not a "literal" translation of *apti simus*. It should be rendered: "that

---

[3] Of dubious attribution, the whole homily is found in PG 43, 439–64.

[4] Anscar Chupungco, "The ICEL2010 Translation," in Edward Foley, gen. ed., *A Commentary on the Order of Mass of The Roman Missal* (Collegeville, MN: Liturgical Press, 2011), 137–38.

[5] Peter Jeffery agrees that "and with your spirit" is preferable (*Translating Tradition: A Chant Historian Reads* Liturgiam Authenticam [Collegeville, MN: Liturgical Press, 2005], 94).

we may be well suited/worthy." The 1998 Missal's third invitation to repentance translates appropriately *both agnoscamus and apti simus*: "My brothers and sisters, let us acknowledge our sins, that we may worthily celebrate these sacred mysteries."[6]

Part of what follows next in the 2010 Missal's translation of the *Confiteor* recalls the obsequious, even cringing language of the imperial courts in Byzantium, Rome, and elsewhere:

> I confess to almighty God and to you, my brothers and sisters,
> that *I have greatly sinned* in my thoughts and in my words,
> in what I have done and in what I have failed to do,
> through my fault, through my fault, *through my most grievous fault*;
> therefore I ask blessed Mary ever-Virgin, all the Angels and Saints,
> and you, my brothers and sisters, to pray for me to the Lord
> our God.
> [emphasis added]

Many of those sharing in the weekly Eucharist find that nothing in their lives corresponds to this confession of their "most grievous fault" and talk about their having "greatly sinned."

Set this 2010 version of the *Confiteor* over against the version given in the 1973 Missal that remained untouched in the 1998 Missal:

> I confess to almighty God, and to you, my brothers and sisters,
> that I have sinned through my own fault, in my thoughts and
> in my words,
> in what I have done, and in what I have failed to do;
> and I ask blessed Mary, ever virgin, all the angels and saints,
> and you, my brothers and sisters, to pray for me to the Lord
> our God.

Sober English replaces the rhetorical, "full-blown" Latin of *nimis peccavi* and *mea culpa, mea culpa, mea maxima culpa*. Everyone today can and should express repentance by simply confessing, "I have sinned through my own fault." This exemplifies the best of English

---

[6] Chupungco, "The ICEL2010 Translation," in Foley, *A Commentary on the Order of Mass*, 138.

understatement and also happily amalgamates "sin" (from *nimis pec-cavi*) and "my own fault" (from *mea culpa, mea culpa, mea maxima culpa*). We find here a helpful example of what Jerome called "changing the style" and Aquinas called "adapting the mode of expression, so that it is in harmony with the idiom of the [receptor] language" (see chapter 2 above).

(4) In its translation of the *Gloria*, the 1998 Missal follows the 1973 Missal word for word, except for replacing "his people on earth" with "God's people on earth." This change, while it also leaves untranslated "the good will" (*bonae voluntatis*) of God, may, nevertheless, appropriately remind us that the peace in question is "God's gift to those he favors," rather than "God's reward to people who possess good will."[7] The translation offered by the 2010 Missal, "Glory to God in the highest, and on earth peace to people of good will," may be more literal, but it has the disadvantage of implying (falsely) that peace is the divine reward to those who possess good will—an example of a Pelagian tendency in this Missal that we will examine later.

Here is the complete translation of the *Gloria* from the 1998 Missal:

> Glory to God in the highest, and peace to God's people on earth.
> Lord God, heavenly King, almighty God and Father,
> we worship you, we give you thanks, we praise you for your
>   glory.
> Lord Jesus Christ, only Son of the Father, Lord God, Lamb of
>   God,
> you take away the sin of the world; have mercy on us;
> you are seated at the right hand of the Father, receive our prayer.
> For you alone are the Holy One, you alone are the Lord,
> you alone are the Most High, Jesus Christ, with the Holy Spirit,
> in the glory of God the Father. Amen.

This translation presents a crescendo (of three words, four words, and six words) in its praise of the first person of the Trinity: "we worship you, we give you thanks, we praise you for your glory." At the same time, this abbreviates the run of five verbs in Latin that also

---

[7] Ibid., 140.

reaches an even more emphatic crescendo: *laudamus te, benedicimus te, adoramus te, glorificamus te, gratias agimus tibi propter magnam gloriam tuam*. In the 1998 translation (and the earlier 1973 translation), *adoramus te* is covered by "we worship you," while *gratias agimus tibi* is rendered in a straightforward way by "we give you thanks." *Laudamus te* is amalgamated with *glorificamus te* and *propter magnam gloriam tuam*, and translated with English brevity: "we praise you for your glory." *Benedicimus te* (we bless you) can be left untranslated, as it is emphatically implied by the three verbs, "we worship you, we give you thanks, we praise you." Worshiping, thanking, and praising are already three forms that blessing God takes. Here the 1998 Missal matches what Peter Jeffery said in chapter 2 about the ancient Roman Rite: so far from insisting on "exact textual renditions, it makes use of omissions and additions."

To be "in harmony" with the "idiom" of English (Aquinas), the 1998 translation tidies up the somewhat repetitive and bombastic source language. Where the Latin original has "Lord Jesus Christ, Only Begotten Son, Lord God, Lamb of God, Son of the Father," the 1998 Missal renders this as: "Lord Jesus Christ, only Son of the Father, Lord God, Lamb of God." "Only Son of the Father" brings together happily "Only Begotten Son" and "Son of the Father." Then six clauses (kept in the 2010 Missal) are neatly reduced to four in the 1998 translation: "you take away the sin of the world, have mercy on us; you are seated at the right hand of the Father, receive our prayer."

In a master stroke the 1998 version brings up to the second line of the *Gloria* "Lord God, heavenly King, almighty God and Father." This identifies clearly whom the hymn addresses when singing: "we worship you, we give you thanks, we praise you for your glory." "The Latin language," as Chupungco points out, "has no strict rules about word order because it enjoys the use of declension. In English, however," it remains unclear and verges on the unintelligible "to recite a series of acclamations whose addressee appears only at the end."[8] But that is what the 2010 Missal does. Here is its version of the *Gloria*, which

----

[8] Ibid., 140–41.

doggedly translates word for word the Latin original and at times finishes up sounding like less than "natural" English (John Henry Newman, Ronald Knox, and George Steiner in chapter 2):

> Glory to God in the highest, and on earth peace to people of
>   good will.
> We praise you, we bless you, we adore you, we glorify you,
> we give you thanks for your great glory.
> Lord God, heavenly King, O God, almighty Father.
> Lord Jesus Christ, Only Begotten Son,
> Lord God, Lamb of God, Son of the Father,
> you take away the sins of the world, have mercy on us;
> you take away the sins of the world, receive our prayer;
> you are seated at the right hand of the Father, have mercy on us.
> [The rest corresponds to what we find above in the 1998 version.]

We have just considered four items in the Introductory Rites; in three cases the 1998 Missal shows itself clearly superior to the 2010 Missal. Chapter 3 has already demonstrated the superiority of the 1998 Missal's translation of the Nicene and Apostles' Creeds, which belong to the Liturgy of the Word. Hence we can move now to the Preparation of the Gifts.

Liturgy of the Eucharist: The Preparation of the Gifts

In the 1998 Missal, the blessing over the bread and the blessing over the wine are made easier to proclaim, and sound more like normal English, by each being broken up into three periods (a shorter, a longer, and a shorter). The first blessing goes as follows: "Blessed are you, Lord, God of all creation. Through your goodness we have this bread to present to you, which earth has given and human hands have made. It will become for us the bread of life." Set this over against the 2010 Missal's one, long sentence, which apes the single, Ciceronian-style sentence of the Latin original: "Blessed are you, Lord God of all creation, for through your goodness we have received the bread we offer you: fruit of the earth and work of human hands, it will become for us the bread of life."

The 2010 Missal insists on translating the Latin *accepimus* (we have received). The 1998 Missal leaves the verb untranslated; obviously it is through the divine goodness that "we have this bread." This translation also rightly leaves untranslated the *quia* (for) of the source language. Once again the reason *for* blessing God is obvious: "we have this bread to present to you."

In line with the official designation for this part of the eucharistic celebration being changed from "the Offertory" to the "Presentation of the Gifts,"[9] the 1998 Missal prefers "present" to "offer" (which had been used in the 1973 translation and is maintained in the 2010 Missal). The meaning of the two verbs overlaps, but the first subtly recalls the official, post–Vatican II heading, "Presentation of the Gifts."

One feature of the 1998 translation that maintains a feature from the 1973 version concerns a difference between the blessing over the bread and the blessing over the wine. The first (see above) speaks of what "earth has given and human hands have made," while it translates the second blessing as "fruit of the vine and work of human hands." It sounds better in English to follow the Latin *fructum vitis* and call wine the "fruit of the vine."[10] And vice versa: it sounds better to call bread that "which earth has given" (*fructum terrae*), rather than "the fruit of the earth," as does the 2010 Missal, which sticks to a literal translation of the Latin original *fructum terrae*. Having used a verb to call bread that "which earth has given," the 1998 version (like that of 1973) rightly introduces a matching verb ("human hands have made") to translate *operis manuum hominum*. In short, the 1998 (like that of 1973) produces better English, while the 2010 Missal doggedly translates word for word, without "caring to write English" (John Henry Newman).

[9] See Patrick Regan, "Theology of the Latin Text and Rite," in Foley, *A Commentary on the Order of Mass*, 211–17, at 211.

[10] This phrase evokes the words of Jesus about not drinking again "the fruit of the vine" until the kingdom of God comes (Mark 14:25; parallels in Matthew and Luke).

Invitation to Prayer

The invitation to prayer, which speaks of *meum ac vestrum sacrificium*, is correctly translated by the 1998 Missal (following that of 1973): "Pray, brothers and sisters, that our sacrifice may be acceptable to God, the almighty Father." The change in the 2010 Missal, "my sacrifice and yours," aimed at expressing a difference between the ordained priesthood and the priesthood of the baptized who make up the assembly. But it does not stand up to scrutiny, either theologically or grammatically.

First, "my sacrifice and yours" is open to be misinterpreted, as if there were two different sacrifices. But, while ordained ministers and the baptized function differently to actualize and express the self-offering of Jesus Christ, there is only one sacrifice in which all are invited to share. All who are united with Christ can and should speak of "our [one] sacrifice."

Second, the authors of the 2010 Missal failed to notice that the Latin text does not say *meum* et *vestrum sacrificium* (my sacrifice and your sacrifice); it uses *ac* rather than *et*. In Latin lexical usage, *et* enumerates. If the Latin original had used *et*, that would mean "my sacrifice and your sacrifice." But *ac* works to connect "nouns, pronouns, and verbs: 'my sacrifice which is also your sacrifice,' or, in short 'our sacrifice.'"[11] Here the 1998 Missal shows its superior grasp of Latin nuances.

The Preface of Eucharistic Prayer II

To evaluate the 1998 Missal's translation of the prefaces, we might take one example and compare it with the corresponding translation in the 2010 Missal. Let me select the 1998 preface that belongs to Eucharistic Prayer II (before going on to examine EPII itself):

> Father, it is our duty and our salvation, always and everywhere,
> to give you thanks through your beloved Son, Jesus Christ. He
> is the Word

[11] Chupungco, "The ICEL2010 Translation," in Foley, *A Commentary on the Order of Mass,* 220.

through whom you made the universe, the Savior you sent to
redeem us.

He took flesh by the Holy Spirit and was born of the Virgin Mary.

To accomplish your will and gain for you a holy people, he
stretched out

his arms on the cross, that he might break the chains of death and
make known the resurrection.

And so with one voice we join the angels and saints in proclaiming
your glory.

Compare this with the version provided by the 2010 Missal, which
follows the Latin rigidly by not breaking up the long opening sentence
(as does the 1998 Missal) and using only three sentences:

It is truly right and just, our duty and our salvation, always and
everywhere

to give you thanks, Father most holy, through your beloved Son,
Jesus Christ, your Word through whom you made all things,
whom you sent as

our Savior and Redeemer, incarnate by the Holy Spirit and born
of the Virgin Mary.

Fulfilling your will and gaining for you a holy people, he
stretched out his hands as he endured his Passion, so as to
break the bonds of death and manifest the resurrection.

And so, with the Angels and all the Saints we declare your glory,
as with one voice we acclaim.

The first difference that catches attention is the way the 1998 translation draws together the meaning of the somewhat wordy Latin: *vere
dignum et justum est, aequum et salutare, nos tibi, sancte Pater.* The
2010 Missal translates word for word. Furthermore, the 1998 version
leaves untranslated *sancte*, since a triple *Sanctus* will be addressed
to God at the end of the preface. The 2010 version changes *sancte* to
sanctissime (most holy), presumably to avoid addressing God in papal
terms as "Holy Father." Yet, when it comes to the opening line of the
anamnesis-offering in the eucharistic prayers for various needs, the

same translation has no such inhibition about translating *Pater sancte* as "holy Father."

The opening protocol in which five christological affirmations appear in apposition to "Jesus Christ" is left as one long, heavy sentence in the 2010 Missal. It is much easier to proclaim the 1998 translation, which breaks the original Latin into three sentences. This translation correctly renders *cuncta* as "the universe," since, unlike *omnia*, *cuncta* tends to have "a collective sense of the whole."[12] "He is the Word through whom you made the universe," followed by "the Savior you sent to redeem us," sets the orders of creation and redemption in beautiful, clear, and sonorous balance. In the Latin, *tuum* (your) qualifies "the Word" but can remain untranslated. Since it was through the Word that God made the universe, the Word is obviously "your Word." Turning the Latin *Redemptorem* into a verb and the dative *nobis* into an accusative "us" is a brilliant touch. The 2010 Missal insists on keeping both nouns, as well as "your," and, within a heavy, excessively long sentence that rigidly follows the Latin word for word, produces two clauses that sound more Latin than English: "your Word through whom you made all things, whom you sent as our Savior and Redeemer." Finally, "Took flesh by the Holy Spirit" is less "technically" theological English (1998 translation) than "incarnate by the Holy Spirit" (2010 Missal).

At the start of the second section of the preface, the 2010 Missal insists on keeping the Latin participles *adimplens* and *acquirens* as "fulfilling your will and gaining for you a holy people." The 1998 translation turns the participles into infinitives and achieves a firmer effect: "to accomplish your will and gain for you a holy people." Then, the Latin text for the preface has *pateretur*, which the 2010 translation, perhaps desiring to match *pateretur* with another word of Latin origin, renders somewhat vaguely as "endured the Passion." The 1998 version gives us the more exact "on the cross." After all it was precisely on the cross that Christ "stretched out his arms" and died. The 2010 Missal's

---

[12] Tom Elich, "The ICEL2010 Translation," in Foley, *A Commentary on the Order of Mass*, 327.

"he stretched out his hands . . . so as to break the bonds of death" does not put things as vividly as "he stretched out his arms . . . that he might break the chains of death" (1998 translation). "Break the chains of death" evokes what the Easter Proclamation (*Exsultet*) sings: "this is the night when Jesus Christ broke the chains of death." For *mortem solveret* (release death's hold) both translations need to supply another noun to go with *mortem*. "Chains" (from the 1998 version) tops the less specific "bonds" (of the 2010 version). In short, "arms," "cross," and "chains" yield a sharper (and more historical) picture than "hands," "Passion," and "bonds."

"Manifest the resurrection" more or less transliterates the Latin *manifestaret* and, consciously or unconsciously, aims at evoking the same verb (*manifestare*) used in the Vulgate for Christ "manifesting" himself risen from the dead (John 21:1, 14). *Manifestare*[13] could be translated by another word of Latin origin that continues to enjoy considerable currency in the media and elsewhere: "reveal."[14] The 1998 translation chooses, however, an accurate rendering of Anglo-Saxon origin, "make known."

Finally, the 2010 translation ends somewhat pompously: "and so, *with* the Angels and all the Saints, we declare [*praedicamus*] your glory, as *with* one voice we acclaim [*dicentes*]" (emphasis added). Avoiding the jarring repetition of "with," the 1998 translation, in fifteen rather than nineteen words, (a) selects a verb ("join") to express our association with the angels and saints, (b) translates *praedicamus* more accurately as "proclaim," and (c) leaves untranslated the participle (*dicentes*) of the colorless verb (*dico*) which merely means "say":

---

[13] In "Theology of the Latin Text and Rite" (in Foley, *A Commentary on the Order of Mass*, 320), the late Irish theologian David Power misses the clear and primary reference to John 21 when he writes: "'*manifestare*' is used in NT Latin [presumably he means the Vulgate] to express the revelation of Christ to the Gentiles, the glory of God shown in Christ, God's revelation through the nativity, the transfiguration and the [Last] Supper, and the glory that the Spirit gives to the Son."

[14] See Gerald O'Collins, *Revelation: Towards a Christian Interpretation of God's Self-revelation in Jesus Christ* (Oxford: Oxford University Press, 2016), 1–2.

"and so with one voice we join the angels and saints in proclaiming your glory."[15]

This is the checklist of differences that once again demonstrate the superiority of the 1998 Missal as a genuine translation from Latin into the receptor language of English. Rather than risk becoming lost in details, some readers may prefer simply to recite aloud the two renderings of the preface and then ask themselves: which of the two translations sounds more like genuine English and so can work better in the setting of the liturgy?

The Sanctus

The 1998 Missal kept the 1973 translation of the *Sanctus*, an "ecumenical" text that can be proclaimed easily and has rightly found its place in the eucharistic liturgies of other churches. This translation remained unchanged in the 2010 Missal, apart from "Lord God of power and might" being unfortunately replaced by "Lord God of hosts." What is the problem here?

The original Hebrew word that completes the Latin title *Dominus Deus Sabaoth* (incorporated in the first line of the *Sanctus*) denotes the armies of angels.[16] The Greek word *stratia* (army) occurs only twice in the New Testament, and both times with this connection. Stephen speaks in Acts 7:42 of *tē stratia tou ouranou* (the army of heaven, the angels as soldiers). In Luke 2:13, we read of the shepherds being confronted with a *plēthos stratias ouraniou*, a phrase happily rendered by the Vulgate as *multitudo militiae caelestis* (a multitude of the heavenly army). This wonderful vision of weapon-bearing angels was preserved in the 1526 translation by William Tyndale: "a multitude of heavenly soldiers."

---

[15] If we "proclaim" with our "voice" the glory of God, we are obviously "saying" something; translating *dicentes* is redundant. At the end of prefaces, the 2010 Missal not only insists on translating "say" but also on doing so with an emphatic "acclaim."

[16] See O'Collins, *Revelation*, 265.

Unfortunately, the King James Bible of 1611 changed this to "a multitude of the heavenly host," a translation followed by twentieth-century translations: "a multitude of the heavenly host" (New Revised Standard Version), and "a great company of the heavenly host" (Revised English Bible).[17] To modern readers of English, "multitude" and "host" often prove more or less synonymous.[18] *Pace* Bruce Harbert,[19] over the centuries "host" has largely lost its military overtones and image of weapon-bearing angels. With its "God of power and might," the 1998 Missal preserves something of these overtones and the original, biblical meaning of *Sabaoth*. But the "Lord God of hosts" of the 2010 Missal, falling unwittingly into line with a loss reflected in modern translations of Luke 2:13, can make people think of God as the God of crowds or multitudes. Or else, without making any connection with the familiar scene of the angels appearing to the shepherds, the congregation can "supply a meaning [for hosts] from their own experience, in this case relating it to hospitality or to particles of bread."[20]

[17] In a footnote to Luke 2:13, the NRSV mentions that the Greek *stratia* means "army." The REB hints at this "military" meaning by replacing "multitude" with "company" and so perhaps recalling that, up to the early seventeenth century, "host" meant an "armed company." But, if so, this would produce the tautology: "a great company of the heavenly armed company."

[18] See how William Wordsworth links "host" with "crowd," itself a near synonym of "multitude," when he writes: "I saw a crowd, a host of golden daffodils . . . Ten thousand saw I at a glance" ("I Wandered Lonely as a Cloud," commonly known as "Daffodils"). I thank Colin Wilcockson for this reference. The *Oxford English Dictionary* defines this meaning of "host" as "a large number of persons or things."

[19] In his *Companion to the Order of Mass*, Harbert states, without any qualification, that hosts "means [present tense] armies" (49). "Host" *used to mean* an "army," but this meaning is listed as "archaic" by the *Oxford English Dictionary*. It now has other meanings: a crowd, those who offer hospitality (as in "the hosts of television programs"), round pieces of bread used at the Eucharist, and so forth. Under "Lord," the OED does, however, list "Lord (God) of Hosts" as meaning "God as Lord over earthly or heavenly armies."

[20] Elich, "The ICEL2010 Translation," in Foley, *A Commentary on the Order of Mass*, 328. On the same page, Elich also draws attention to another, serious loss caused by the changed translation of the *Sanctus* in the 2010 Missal: Catholics

The Post-Sanctus *of the Second Eucharistic Prayer*

The 2010 Missal translates the brief *Post-Sanctus*: "You are indeed holy, O Lord, the fount of all holiness." Compare this with the 1998 translation: "Lord, you are holy indeed, you are the fountain of all holiness." Here the sentence clarifies at once the addressee, "Lord," without the unnecessary and slightly pompous "O," which is not found in the Latin original. "You" is repeated, so as to emphasize that God is both holy as such and also the source of all other holiness.

As regards a second difference, Elich comments: "'fountain' [which was already found in the 1973 Missal] might be mistaken for an item of decorative landscaping." He welcomes the shift to "fount, with its evocation of a spring or source."[21] I wonder whether the shift is for the good. After all, the Scriptures (and contemporary English) use "fountain" to express a spring or source and not merely a decoration in some landscape. The psalmist addresses God: "with you is the fountain of life." This fountain is the equivalent of "the river of your delights," from which worshipers drink (Ps 36:8-9). Wisdom is "a fountain of life" (Prov 16:22). "Fount" is a back-formation from "fountain," like "mount" from "mountain." In the *Post-Sanctus* "you are the fountain of all holiness" concludes with two words that both share a similar strength. "The fount of all holiness" seems to scurry over the first noun and give a little too much emphasis to "all holiness."

For Sundays in Ordinary Time, the 1998 Missal has added a prayer to give a little more weight to the brief *Post-Sanctus* and introduce more solemnly the epiclesis: "*In communion* with the whole Church, we have assembled on this day which you have *made holy*, and, rejoicing that you have made us a *new creation* in your risen Son, we pray . . ." (emphasis added). At this point, for Eucharistic Prayer III, the same 1998 Missal has added seven *communicantes*, which belong, respectively, to the seasons of Advent, Christmas, the Epiphany, Lent, Easter, the Ascension, and Pentecost. These seven prayers imitate Eu-

---

are made to abandon a "common ecumenical text we have shared with other churches." This loss does not appear to concern Monsignor Harbert or the author(s) of *Liturgiam Authenticam*.

[21] Ibid.

charistic Prayer I, which traditionally had five proper *communicantes* (for Christmas, the Epiphany, Easter, the Ascension, and Pentecost). We return to the *Post-Sanctus* of Eucharistic Prayer II. (a) The lines added in the 1998 Missal pick up Paul's teaching about the "new creation" (2 Cor 5:17). (b) The language about being "in communion with the whole Church" evokes the *communicantes* (found for centuries in the classic Roman Canon, now called Eucharistic Prayer I) and expresses the desire to be associated with the whole living Church, including those who have already entered into glory. (c) The day that God has "made holy" continues the central theme of the *Post-Sanctus* and introduces what is to come in the invocation of the Holy Spirit (the epiclesis).

The Epiclesis

Eight words in the original Latin form the opening lines of the epiclesis: *Haec ergo dona, quaesumus, Spiritus tui rore sanctifica.* Joyce Ann Zimmerman, director of the Institute for Liturgical Ministry in Dayton, Ohio, appreciates the life-giving nourishment conveyed through the image "by the dew of your Spirit" (*Spiritus tui rore*). She recalls the layer of dew that left fragments of manna to nourish the Israelites in the wilderness (Exod 16:13-15).[22] David Power points out, however, that while dew is used as a metaphor for divine action (for example, Isa 45:8), nowhere in the biblical Latin of the Vulgate is dew associated precisely with the action of the Spirit. As for liturgical Latin, it "usually uses the words *virtute* or *gratia* when referring to the workings of the Spirit."[23] It seems that the image "by the dew of your Spirit" came from those who after Vatican II composed Eucharistic Prayer II rather than from the anaphora of the ancient *Apostolic Tradition* that was the inspiration of this Eucharistic Prayer.[24]

[22] J. A. Zimmerman, "The Mystagogical Implications," in Foley, *A Commentary on the Order of Mass*, 337.

[23] Power, "Theology of the Latin Text and Rite," in Foley, *A Commentary on the Order of Mass*, 321; curiously he misses the reference to dew in Exodus 16, which Zimmerman quotes.

[24] See John Baldovin, "History of the Latin Text and Rite," in Foley, *A Commentary on the Order of Mass*, 311–16.

The 1998 translation (eleven words) flows easily: "send down your Spirit upon these gifts to make them holy." Two words in the Latin text, *ergo* and *quaesumus*, belong more to the idiom of ancient Latin and are left untranslated. The words "send down" pick up something of the image of dew falling on the gifts of bread and wine to make them spiritually nourishing and sanctifying for the communicants. But the precise "dewfall of the Spirit," alien to modern English as it was to biblical and liturgical Latin, is left untranslated.

The 2010 translation runs as follows: "Make holy, therefore, these gifts, we pray, by sending down your Spirit upon them like the dewfall." This rendering preserves the unnecessary "therefore" and the obsequious "we pray." The result involves taking seventeen words to translate eight words in Latin. Tom Elich notices how "the four discrete phrases ("make holy, therefore, these gifts, we pray") could encourage an ugly "staccato proclamation." He characterizes as "wordy and prosaic" what follows: "by sending down your Spirit upon them like the dewfall."[25]

The Institution Narrative

The 1998 translation shows itself superior in its version of the words over the bread and, even more, in its version of the words over the wine. The words over the bread are as follows: "Before he was *given up* to death, a death he freely accepted, he took bread and gave you thanks; he broke the bread, gave it to his disciples, and said: 'TAKE THIS, ALL OF YOU, AND EAT IT: THIS IS MY BODY, WHICH WILL BE *GIVEN UP* FOR YOU'" (emphasis added). The same Latin verb *tradere* is used here twice: Christ "was given up to death" and his body would be "given up for you." This verb corresponds to a verb used persistently by Mark in his story of Jesus' final suffering: *paradidōmi* (give up, hand over)—from Mark 14:10 to 15:15. As Elich comments, it is "worth preserving in translation" the "significant verbal parallel between table and cross."[26] Others (Judas, the chief priests and their collaborators, and then Pilate) give Jesus up to suffering and death

---

[25] Elich, "The ICEL2010 Translation," in Foley, *A Commentary on the Order of Mass*, 329.

[26] Ibid.

on the cross. But he has already "given himself up" by the words of institution at the table of the Last Supper, and Paul will speak of God the Father, out of love "for all of us," "giving his Son up" (Rom 8:32).

This significant verbal parallel in the use of *tradere* goes lost in the 2010 translation. It renders the opening words as "at the time he was betrayed" and the words over the bread as "which will be given up for you." The verb is the same in the original Latin. It is strange that a translation based on literal, word-for-word translation could slip up in this fashion by varying the translation within the space of a few lines and so hiding the connection and contrast between Judas giving Christ up and Christ giving himself up.

When we come to the words pronounced over the wine, the differences between the 1998 and the 2010 translations prove more serious. The 1998 translation gives us: "When supper was ended, he took *the cup*, again he gave you thanks, gave *the cup* to his disciples, and said: TAKE THIS, ALL OF YOU, AND DRINK FROM IT: THIS IS *THE CUP* OF MY BLOOD, THE BLOOD OF THE NEW AND EVERLASTING COVENANT. IT WILL BE *SHED* FOR YOU AND *FOR ALL*, SO THAT SINS MAY BE FORGIVEN. DO THIS IN MEMORY OF ME" (emphasis added). Three items set this translation apart from the 2010 Missal, which uses "chalice" (instead of "cup"), "poured" (instead of "shed"), and "for many" (instead of "for all").

First, Gilbert Ostdiek, a professor of liturgy at Catholic Theological Union in Chicago, observes that all the New Testament accounts of the institution of the Eucharist (Matt 26:27; Mark 14:23; Luke 22:20; 1 Cor 11:25-26) have *potērion*, which in first-century Greek meant "cup." It is so translated by all the major English versions of the New Testament (the Authorized Version, the New American Bible, the New Jerusalem Bible, the New Revised Standard Version, the Revised English Bible, and the Revised Standard Version). In the Latin of the Vulgate version and, specifically, in the four accounts of the institution, *potērion* was translated as *calix*, but, at that time, this noun simply meant "cup" (especially, for holding wine) or "drinking vessel."[27] In the

---

[27] See Gilbert Ostdiek, "The ICEL2010 Translation," in Foley, *A Commentary on the Order of Mass*, 287. See "calix" in P. D. W. Glare, ed., *Oxford Latin Dictionary*

mystagogical lectures of St. Ambrose of Milan (d. 397), we have the first evidence for the Roman Canon, and it speaks of Christ "taking the cup."[28] The word in Ambrose's text was *calicem*, which, as in the Vulgate, meant "cup" and not "chalice," as used in later, ecclesiastical Latin to denote an ornamented drinking vessel reserved for use in the eucharistic liturgy. By choosing a now "sacred" word ("chalice") over a more general word ("cup"), the translators who produced the 2010 Missal have proved inaccurate and anachronistic—in terms of both the New Testament and the early Christian tradition of the Vulgate and the Roman Canon.[29]

Second, those translators also preferred to render *effundere* as "poured out" rather than "shed." But this involved losing what the verb suggested in the context of the institution narrative. Anscar Chupungco explains the difference: "To pour out" can "simply mean to empty out . . . expressing volubly and at length one's feelings of anger or sorrow. Unlike the verb 'to shed' (shed tears, shed blood), 'to pour out' does not necessarily suggest sacrifice or suffering." Hence he argues: "In the context of the Last Supper of Jesus, 'effundere' has a decidedly sacrificial undertone, which should not be passed over in translation." In the 1998 Missal, which followed here the 1973 translation, it was correct to choose the strong verb "to shed" ("it will be shed for you and for all"). At this point the 2010 Missal by choosing "pour out" weakens "the theology of Eucharistic sacrifice."[30]

The choice also ignores some biblical translations of the institution narratives. The original Greek of Matthew 26:28, Mark 14:24, and Luke 22:20 all use a participle *ekchunnomenon* formed from the verb

---

(Oxford: Clarendon Press, 1982); and Thomas O'Loughlin, "The Liturgical Vessels of the Latin Eucharist: A Case of an Embedded Theology," *Worship* 82 (2008): 482–504, at 488–94.

[28] See John Baldovin, "History of the Latin Text and Rite," in Foley, *A Commentary on the Order of Mass*, 248.

[29] As many have pointed out, the 2010 translation is inconsistent when it uses "cup" and not "chalice" in the second acclamation: "When we eat this Bread and drink this Cup, we proclaim your Death, O Lord, until you come again."

[30] Chupungco, "EP RI: The ICEL2010 Translation," in Foley, *A Commentary on the Order of Mass*, 480.

ekchunnomai, which can mean "to shed" as well as "to pour out." One major translation (the New American Bible) reveals a sensitivity to the sacrificial context and adopts "shed" for all three of these verses. The Revised English Bible also uses "shed," at least in the case of Matthew 26:28 and Mark 14:24. Here some translators of the gospels show more theological insight than those who translated liturgical texts for the 2010 Missal.

In this context one should also recall one of the classic statements in the New Testament that concerns the blood of Christ: "without the shedding of blood [*haimatekchusias*] there is no forgiveness/remission of sins" (Heb 9:22). Formed from the verb *ekchunnomai* (or from the related and synonymous verb *ekcheō*), this noun is translated as "shedding of blood" (and not "pouring out of blood") not only by the New American Bible and the Revised English Bible, but also by the New Jerusalem Bible, the New Revised Standard Version, and the Revised Standard Version. Here more translators show themselves sensitive to the sacrificial overtones of the New Testament language.

Third, we come to what Chupungco has called "probably the most regrettable example of a slavish application of literal translation" in the entire 2010 Missal: Christ's blood being "poured out for you and for many" (and not "for all").[31] At the end of chapter 3, we presented at length the case against changing to "for many." In Isaiah 53, Romans 5, and elsewhere in the New Testament, the original "for many" in Hebrew and Greek has a collective and not a restrictive sense: it means "for all." At the Last Supper, Christ intended the redemption of "all," whether or not every individual was to take up his saving offer. "For many" is misleading; it seems to limit the scope of Jesus' intention to save all. Harbert comments: "[for many] should not be taken to imply that Christ did not die for all human beings."[32] In other words, in the context of the institution narrative, "for many" means "for all." Why not express the true meaning and clearly avoid risk of false theology by maintaining the translation "for all"? In short, if X ("for many") means Y ("for all"), should we not translate the phrase as Y? Here and

---

[31] Ibid., 481.
[32] Harbert, *Companion to the Order of Mass*, 61.

elsewhere, Harbert shows himself ready to have the English text say one thing but mean another.[33]

Acclamations

In the liturgical reform of the Roman Rite that followed the Second Vatican Council, acclamations, usually addressed to the risen Christ, were added at this point. This was to follow the practice of Eastern rites and, in particular, the Liturgy of St. James. After the words of institution, the people responded with wonder to the mystery of Christ present to them. By confessing the mystery, they were enabled to share in it and live by it.

Where the 1973 Missal invited the people's acclamation by the priest or deacon saying or singing, "Let us proclaim the mystery of faith," the 2010 Missal pares the invitation down to an exact translation of the Latin text that, however, sounds abrupt in English: "The mystery of faith." The 1998 Missal first proposes, however, an invitation that returns to the text of 1 Timothy 3:16: "great is the mystery of faith." The people then take up this acclamation by saying or singing: "Christ has died, Christ is risen, Christ will come again." This response, an original ICEL composition already found in the 1973 Missal, became popular, but was dropped from the 2010 Missal because of the inflexible rule that the Latin text of the 1970 Missal was to be translated without any additions (*Liturgiam Authenticam*, 98, 106).

The 1998 Missal then offers three alternative acclamations, all superior to their matching counterparts in the 2010 Missal. In answer to "Praise to you, Lord Jesus," the people acclaim: "Dying you destroyed our death, rising you restored our life. Lord Jesus, come in glory." This acclamation, already proposed by the 1973 Missal, makes richer sense than the 2010 Missal's word-for-word translation: "We proclaim your Death, O Lord, and profess your Resurrection, until you come again."

Unlike the 1973 version followed by that of 1998, which specifies matters of identity by expanding the translation to "Lord Jesus," the 2010 Missal sticks to the bare "Lord" (*Domine*), a title used for

---

[33] See n. 19 above.

all three Persons of the Trinity. Apart from being distracted by the capitalization ("Death" and "Resurrection"), one is left asking: why should we proclaim this death and profess this resurrection—a question answered by the 1973/1998 "you destroyed our death" and "you restored our life"? In any case, the 2010 rendering can hardly claim to be a literal translation, since the Latin *donec venias* becomes "until you come *again*" (emphasis added). "Again" is an expansion, and a less than vivid expansion than "come *in glory*" of the 1973/1998 acclamation (emphasis added).

The further alternative acclamation in the 1998 Missal brings together words of John and Paul. The deacon or priest, echoing the eucharistic discourse of John 6, sings or says, "Christ is the bread of life." The people, echoing 1 Corinthians 11:26, respond: "When we eat this bread and drink this cup, we proclaim your death, Lord Jesus, until you come in glory." "This bread" picks up the language of the invitation, "Christ is the bread of life." Compare the acclamation with the 2010 translation: "When we eat this Bread and drink this Cup, we proclaim your Death, O Lord, until you come again." This translation adds three capitals, a second "this," "O," and "again," none of which is present in the Latin original text. So much for an allegedly word-for-word translation!

A final alternative in the 1998 Missal begins with words from 1 Corinthians 12: "Jesus Christ is Lord." The people's acclamation repeats the final word, and says: "Lord, by your cross and resurrection you have set us free. You are the Savior of the world." This avoids an apparent non sequitur in the original Latin: *Salvator mundi, salva nos, qui per crucem et resurrectionem tuam liberasti nos*. Why pray to be saved, if the Savior of the world has already set us free through his cross and resurrection? The apparent non sequitur becomes more blatant in the 2010 translation, which reads the (relative pronoun) *qui* as if it were (a conjunction) *quia* and gives us: "Save us, Savior of the world, for by your Cross and Resurrection you have set us free." Why pray to be saved by the Savior of the world, since he has already set us free? Once again we are also distracted by a capitalization, "Cross and Resurrection," which is not present in the Latin original.

If we were to press on to check the rest of Eucharistic Prayer II in the two versions, from 1998 and 2010, respectively, we could easily spot various advantages in the former and defects in the latter translation. Some comments from Tom Elich would offer a good place to start this comparing and contrasting.[34]

In particular, he draws attention to the theologically deft 1973/1998 translation of *aeternae vitae mereamur esse consortes*: "make us worthy to share eternal life with Mary" and so forth. The 2010 version ("we may merit to be coheirs to eternal life") suggests that eternal salvation comes through our own merits and not, primarily, through the grace of God.[35]

In support of the translation (which reveals a Pelagian conviction) "we may merit to be coheirs to eternal life," Cuthbert Johnson quotes Paul: "now if we are children, then we are heirs, heirs of God and coheirs of Christ" (Rom 8:17).[36] The apostle would be horrified to be named as someone who expounds the notion of "meriting to be coheirs to eternal life." In Romans 8, he understands us to be coheirs of Christ, not because of something we have done and merited, but because we have received adoption as God's sons and daughters (Rom 8:14-16).

The Communion Rite

To complete this sampling of the 1998 translation, let us take up some items from the Communion Rite and the Concluding Rite. This translation renders brilliantly the invitation to the Lord's Prayer provided by the Latin original: "Taught by the Savior's command and formed by the word of God, we dare to say" (*Praeceptis salutaribus moniti, et divina institutione formati, audemus dicere*). It also offers four other appropriate invitations: for instance, "Let us pray for the coming of the kingdom as Jesus taught us." The 2010 Missal allows for no such alternatives, and translates: "At the Savior's command and formed by divine teaching, we dare to say." This resembles the 1998 translation by rendering more personally the *praeceptis salutaribus* (saving precepts), but it lacks the firm and balanced structure provided by two participles, "*taught* by the Savior's command and *formed* by the word of God." "By divine

---

[34] Elich, "The ICEL2010 Translation," in Foley, *A Commentary on the Order of Mass,* 331–34.

[35] Ibid., 334.

[36] Johnson, *Understanding the Roman Missal,* 62.

teaching" limps behind "by the word of God," which happily evokes "the liturgy of the word," with which the service has begun.

The 1998 Missal then presents the Lord's Prayer in a 1975 rendering that came from an ecumenical commission, the International Consultation on English Texts (ICET): "Our Father in heaven, hallowed be your name, your kingdom come, your will be done on earth as in heaven. Give us today our daily bread. Forgive us our sins as we forgive those who sin against us. Save us from the time of trial and deliver us from evil." In a slightly different, earlier form (for example, in India, the Philippines, and other Asian countries) and then in the 1975 form (in New Zealand, for example), this text had been adopted by English-speaking Catholic communities. It was widely hoped that this version might achieve an ecumenical consensus.[37]

The 2010 Missal chose, however, the traditional form of the Lord's Prayer, which, with slight modifications, goes back to the sixteenth-century *Book of Common Prayer.* That choice lost the opportunity to express the central prayer of Christianity "in contemporary and unambiguous language"[38] that might be adopted by all Christians. The preparation of the 2010 Missal was once again hampered by *Liturgiam Authenticam* excluding ecumenical collaboration in the work of translation (LA 98).

The "embolism" or elaboration of the Lord's Prayer follows. The 1998 Missal breaks up the one, long sentence of the Latin original: "Deliver us, Lord, from every evil, and grant us peace in our day. In your mercy keep us free from sin and protect us in the time of trial, as we wait in joyful hope for the coming of our Savior, Jesus Christ." The translation follows the 1973 Missal, except for replacing "from all anxiety" with "in the time of trial." This change deftly recalls "save us from the time of trial" in the version of the Lord's Prayer that has been introduced.

Set this rendering of the embolism over against the 2010 Missal's version, which doggedly maintains the long sentence and the obsequious "we pray" (*quaesumus*) and "graciously" (*propitius*), which belong to Ciceronian and classical liturgical Latin, but not to modern

---

[37] See Elich, "The ICEL2010 Translation," in Foley, *A Commentary on the Order of Mass,* 607–9.

[38] Ibid., 614.

English. "Deliver us, Lord, *we pray*, from every evil, *graciously* grant peace in our days, that by the help of your mercy, we may be always free from sin and safe from all distress, as we await the blessed hope and the coming of our Savior Jesus Christ" (emphasis added).[39] This translation takes forty-seven words to say what the 1998 Missal says in forty-two and the original Latin in thirty-eight.

We can observe something similar when we compare the two versions of the prayer for peace. In the 1998 version, "Lord Jesus Christ, you said to your apostles: Peace I leave with you, my peace I give to you. [This replaces the 1973 translation: 'I leave you peace, my peace I give you.'] Look not on our sins, but on the faith of your Church, and grant us the peace and unity of your kingdom, where you live for ever and ever." The verb "grant" sums up neatly the meaning of *secundum voluntatem tuam* (according to your will) . . . *digneris* (consider worthy)." To consider worthy "according to your will" is simply a case of classical liturgical Latin saying in a fulsome way: "grant."

The 2010 version remains locked into a breathless, Latin sentence and also insists on twice maintaining the relative pronoun *qui*. "Lord Jesus Christ, *who* [*qui*] said to your Apostles: Peace I leave you, my peace I give you, look not on our sins, but on the faith of your Church, and graciously grant [*digneris*] her peace and unity in accordance with your will, *Who* [*qui*] live and reign for ever and ever." The prayer turns ponderous, from "graciously grant" right through to the end. Taking the Latin text word for word, it translates *vivis et regnas* quite literally as "live and reign." Here the 1998 version follows that of 1973 by turning the verb *regnas* into the appropriate noun "kingdom."

There are three formulas offered by the 1998 translation for inviting the people to exchange a sign of peace. It also allows the priest or deacon to use "similar words." The 2010 Missal includes, however, no such options, and flatly prescribes, "Let us offer each other the sign of

---

[39] In an earlier version, there was no "and" but a comma after "the blessed hope." This allowed "the blessed hope" to be explained by "the coming of our Savior." Introducing, in slavish deference to the original Latin, an "and" after "the blessed hope," the final translation of 2010 implies that there are two different realities to be expected. Hearers could be mystified about a "blessed hope," distinct from "the coming of our Savior." See ibid., 610.

peace." A similar poverty is apparent at the *Agnus Dei*, which leads off the breaking of the bread; this Missal provides no alternatives. The 1998 translation offers, however, a variety for the invocations of Jesus not only as the "Lamb of God," but also as "Bread of Life," "Prince of Peace," and so forth.

When it reaches the invitation to receive Holy Communion, the 1998 Missal provides three possible formulas, the first being: "Behold the Lamb of God, who takes away the sin of the world. Blessed are those called to the banquet of the Lamb." The people respond: "Lord, I am not worthy to receive you, but only say the word and I shall be healed." "The sin [in the singular] of the world" matches exactly the words of John the Baptist about the Lamb of God "who takes away the sin of the world" (John 1:29). It corrects the plural, "sins" (*peccata*), which was not present in the accurate Vulgate translation (*Ecce Agnus Dei qui tollit peccatum mundi*) but had crept into Latin liturgical texts. The "banquet of the Lamb" picks up Revelation 19:9 and the call to the heavenly banquet where the Lamb of God is enthroned.

The 2010 Missal maintains the double "behold" (*ecce*) found in the Latin original and the plural ("sins"): "*Behold* the Lamb of God, *behold* him who takes away the *sins* of the world. Blessed are those called to the supper of the Lamb" (emphasis added). The people respond with the priest: "Lord, I am not worthy that you should enter under my roof (*sub tectum meum*), but only say the word and my soul (*anima mea*) shall be healed." Despite the clear reference to Revelation and the heavenly banquet, this translation prefers "supper of the Lamb," presumably to establish a clear reference to the Lord's Supper (1 Cor 11:20).

The response recalls language used in the story of the centurion's sick servant being healed (Matt 8:5-13). Elich points out a danger with the phrase "enter under my roof": "people may take it at face value and think 'the roof of my mouth.' This is not just a quaint misunderstanding but could [also] lead to an unhelpful theology, limiting and localizing the real presence of the living, risen Christ in the Blessed Sacrament."[40] People might also easily think that Holy Communion brings the healing of the soul and not the deep healing of the whole

---

[40] Ibid., 613.

person. Of course, "soul" used to mean the whole person, as in "the ship went down, with the loss of all souls." But in contemporary English "soul" may seem to endorse a misleading dualism of body and soul. "I shall be healed" avoids this problem and expresses the meaning of the Latin *sanabitur anima mea.* "I shall be healed" also fits better the story of the centurion's servant. It was his body that was healed and not his soul. His spiritual healing was not the issue.

Concluding Rite

Two simple blessings are offered by the 1998 Missal: "May almighty God bless you, the Father, and the Son, and the Holy Spirit." And then: "May the blessing of almighty God, the Father, and the Son, and the Holy Spirit, come down upon you and remain with you forever." The 2010 Missal provides the first but reserves the second for occasions when the final blessing is preceded by a more solemn formula or by a prayer over the people.

Three formulas for dismissal are found in the 1998 Order of Mass: "go in peace to love and serve the Lord"; "go in the peace of Christ"; and "the Mass is ended, go in peace." The 1973 Missal already contained all three formulas. But what had taken third place is moved to first place: "go in peace to love and serve the Lord." This dismissal had proved itself in practice and become very popular.

The 2010 Missal drops this and the other two formulas, offering a choice between four formulas: (1) "Go forth, the Mass is ended" (which approximates most closely the Latin *Ite missa est*); (2) "Go and announce the Gospel of the Lord"; (3) "Go in peace, glorifying the Lord by your life"; and simply (4) "Go in peace." The second and third formulas introduce useful alliteration: "Go . . . Gospel," and "Go . . . glorifying." The second formula would have been more powerful if it ran: "Go out to announce the Gospel of the Lord."[41]

Judgments will vary. But, it seems to me, the three formulas provided by the 1998 Missal trump the four provided by the 2010 Missal. Let us turn now to a feature of the 1998 Missal that shows its clear superiority: the opening prayers.

---

[41] Ibid., 643.

Chapter Five

The Opening Prayers of the 1998 Missal

*I*n chapter 1 of this book, John Wilkins praised the opening prayers or (as they are still often called) "collects" offered by the 1998 Missal. They improved dramatically on those offered in the 1973 Missal and tower over the stodgy, heavy translations in the "halfway," word-for-word English of the 2010 Missal. Members of the old ICEL were rightly proud of what they had achieved in capturing the biblical echoes and theological implications of the collects and in expressing them in very intelligible English.

The remit that ICEL had received from the English-speaking bishops' conferences included the task of providing some original texts, or texts not translated from the Latin 1970 *Missale Romanum* but composed expressly for the Missal in English. The Vatican instruction of 1969, *Comme le prévoit*, as we noted in chapter 2, considered the "creation" of such new texts to be "necessary" (CLP 43). The 1973 Missal already offered some examples of such "original texts." They were also found in the official translations of the 1970 Missal into some non-English languages that received the required *recognitio* from the Holy See.[1]

Encouraged by their remit from English-speaking bishops and by the guidelines of *Comme le prévoit*, ICEL not only translated the

---

[1] *Liturgiam Authenticam* (LA 106–7) allowed for the composition of new texts, hedged about with various qualifications. But, in fact, no original texts in English were created for the 2010 Missal, apart from three new formulas for "dismissal" at the end of Mass.

collects in the *Missale Romanum* of 1970 but also crafted "alternatives," opening prayers inspired by the biblical readings prescribed for the Sundays in years A, B, and C, respectively. Hence for each Sunday of the year, the 1998 Missal supplies three alternative opening prayers,[2] along with a translation of the collect (drawn from ancient Latin sources) provided by the 1970 *Missale Romanum.*[3]

This chapter will explore in detail sixteen collects or opening prayers from the 1998 Missal: four translations from the 1970 *Missale Romanum* and twelve newly composed "alternative" prayers. These sixteen collects come from two Sundays of Advent and two Sundays of Ordinary Time—four collects from each of the four Sundays.

We begin with samples from Advent: the opening prayers translated from the Latin original and the corresponding three alternatives composed in English.

The First Sunday of Advent

For the First Sunday of Advent, the Latin opening prayer in the 1970 *Missale Romanum* goes as follows: "Da, quaesumus, omnipotens Deus, hanc tuis fidelibus voluntatem, ut, Christo tuo venienti iustis operibus occurrentes, eius dexterae sociati, regnum mereantur possidere caeleste."

The 1973 Missal translated this: "All-powerful God, increase our strength of will for doing good, that Christ may find an eager welcome at his coming and call us to his side in the kingdom of heaven." This left untranslated the initial, unnecessary, and obsequious *quaesumus* (we pray). But it played down the classical resonances of *tuis fidelibus* (your faithful) by turning them into the bland "our" and "us." "For doing good" is likewise bland and general, leaving behind any of the specificity conveyed by *iustis operibus* (works of justice). The "your"

---

[2] The 1998 Missal also supplies some alternative opening prayers for feasts of the Lord and the saints.

[3] Gerard Moore, an Australian liturgist, has provided a meticulous study of the origins and meaning of ancient collects chosen for the 1970 *Missale Romanum*: *Vatican II and the Collects for Ordinary Time* (Bethesda, MD: International Scholars Publications, 1998).

in the freshly personal *Christo tuo* (your Christ) remains untranslated. Three Latin verbs (*sociati, mereantur,* and *possidere*) are amalgamated into one verb, "call." Finally, "at his side" is less specific than "at his right hand" (*dexterae*), which features in Matthew's scene of final judgment when Christ will call to his *right hand* "the blessed of my Father" (Matt 25:33-34).

The 1998 Missal provides this highly successful translation:

> Almighty God, strengthen the resolve of your faithful people
> to prepare for
> the coming of your Christ by works of justice and mercy,
> so that when we go forth to meet him, he may call us to sit at
> his right hand
> and possess the kingdom of heaven.
> We ask this through our Lord Jesus Christ, your Son, who lives
> and reigns
> with you in the unity of the Holy Spirit, God for ever and ever.

Let us examine the achievement in detail. Where the 1973 Missal had "increase our strength of will," the 1998 Missal renders more accurately the original Latin, *da . . . hanc tuis fidelibus voluntatem,* with its "strengthen the resolve of your faithful people." Only then will it personalize "your people" as "*we* go forth" and "call *us.*" What is implicit in the Latin text is made explicit by adding "to prepare for." This secures a neat balance between what is done now (preparing for the coming of your Christ) and what will happen then (going forth to meet him, *occurrentes*). By expanding *iustis operibus* to "works of justice *and mercy,*" the prayer secures a firmer link to the corporal works of mercy that provide the standard for the final judgment described in Matthew. The 1998 Missal keeps the verb "call," which corresponds to what the King will say to the blessed who at judgment are placed "at his right hand" (Matt 25:34). The prayer achieves a pleasing balance by adding "sit" (implied in the Latin original) and by translating *possedere.* The faithful will be called "to sit at his right hand and possess the kingdom of heaven." Finally, the collect finds a proper, English place for the initial "we ask" (*quaesumus*). It is used at the end and to start a separate sentence: "We ask this through our Lord Jesus Christ."

By comparison, the 2010 Missal renders this opening prayer as follows: "Grant your faithful, we pray, almighty God, the resolve to run forth to meet your Christ with righteous deeds at his coming, so that, gathered at his right hand, they may be worthy to possess the heavenly Kingdom. Through our Lord Jesus Christ."

The somewhat odd picture emerges here of a "resolve to run forth to meet your Christ with righteous deeds at his coming." When Christ comes at the end, it will be too late for such a resolve to engage in any righteous deeds and run forth with them to meet Christ. But that is the impression conveyed by the 2010 Missal. It forgets that the timing for all human deeds is earlier, during the preparation for Christ's coming, as is clear in Matthew's scene of the judgment of the nations. The blessed have *already* engaged in deeds of mercy before Christ comes on the scene in final judgment. The 1998 Missal makes it clear when the resolve to engage in works of justice and mercy can have its effect—during the time of preparation for Christ's final coming. By praying that God may "call us to sit at his right hand" and so "possess the kingdom of God," the 1998 translation ensures respect for the prior, divine initiative. The 2010 translation, as too often elsewhere, obscures this central truth and makes it sound as if it is our worthiness that makes us merit the kingdom of heaven. There are other defects. In the Latin original, *regnum* is in lower case, but this translation insists on introducing a capital letter, "Kingdom." Finally, by inserting a period after "Kingdom" and moving to "Through our Lord Jesus Christ," this translation produces a final sentence that lacks a verb. How much better is the 1998 version: "We ask this through our Lord Jesus Christ"!

Let us turn now to *the alternative opening prayers* that the 1998 Missal provides for Years A, B, and C. The Bible readings for *Year A* are as follows: Isaiah 2:1-5; Romans 13:11-14; Matthew 24:37-44. These readings are matched by this alternative opening prayer:

> God of majesty and power, amid the clamor of our violence
> your Word of Truth resounds; upon a world made dark by sin
>   the Sun of Justice casts his dawning rays.

Keep your household watchful and aware of the hour in which
we live.

Hasten the advent of that day when the sounds of war will be
for ever stilled,

the darkness of evil scattered, and all your children gathered
into one.

We ask this through him whose coming is certain, whose day
draws near:

your Son, our Lord Jesus Christ, who lives and reigns with you
in the unity of the Holy Spirit, God for ever and ever.

The wording is superb. Let me offer four comments. First, the reading from Isaiah opens by directing attention to "days to come." The
alternative prayer asks for "the advent of that day" and speaks of the
"day" that "draws near." The same reading from Isaiah ends by inviting the people to walk "in the light of the Lord." The image of light
turns up in this alternative prayer, with "the Sun of Justice" casting
"his dawning rays." But the major connection between reading and
prayer is made by Isaiah announcing that "swords" will be "beaten
into plowshares" and "spears into pruning hooks. Nation shall not lift
up sword against nation, neither shall they learn war any more." The
alternative prayer resonates with this hope by evoking "the clamor
of our violence" and the "day when the sounds of war will be for ever
stilled." As "the Word of truth resounds," the clamor of violence and
the sounds of war will give way to the peaceful clang of swords and
spears being forged into peaceful, agricultural tools.[4]

Second, the passage from Paul's Letter to the Romans supplies the
language of time and waking from sleep: "you know what *time* it is,
how it is *now* the *moment* for you to *wake from sleep*. For salvation
is *nearer* to us than *when* we became believers; the night is *far gone*,
the day is *near*." The prayer takes up the theme of time: "Keep your
household *watchful* and *aware* of the *hour* in which we live. *Hasten*

---

[4] A major theme in the passage from Isaiah concerns Jerusalem uniting peoples
of all lands; they come together there for instruction. The prayer briefly touches
this theme with its words about "all your children gathered into one."

the *advent* of that day *when* . . ." The prayer is made "through him whose *coming* is certain, whose day *draws near*" (emphasis added).

Time and watchfulness link Paul and the prayer, but the contrast of darkness and light provides perhaps a stronger link. The apostle writes: "the *night* is far gone, the *day* is near. Let us then lay aside the works of *darkness* and put on the armor of *light*. Let us live honorably as in the *day*." That provides major imagery for the alternative prayer for the First Sunday of Advent in Year A: "upon a world *made dark* by sin the *Sun* of Justice casts his *dawning rays*" (emphasis added). It asks God to "hasten the advent of that day" when "the darkness of evil" will be "scattered."

Third, the full impact of the passage from Matthew comes at its close: "Keep awake . . . for you do not know on what day your Lord is coming . . . if the owner of the house had known in which part of the night the thief was coming, he would have stayed awake. . . . You must be ready, for the Son of Man is coming at an unexpected hour." The prayer picks up this message: "*Keep* your *household watchful* and aware of the *hour* in which we live" (emphasis added).

Fourth, over and beyond the biblical language and imagery that color it, this prayer enjoys an elegant structure that can be effectively proclaimed. After invoking the "God of majesty and power," it presents the setting in which Christ (described with two titles, "your Word of Truth" and "Sun of Justice") is active as the agent of divine revelation: "amid the clamor of our violence your Word of Truth resounds; upon a world made dark by sin the Sun of Justice casts his dawning rays." The second part of the prayer sketches in three finely crafted clauses something of what redemption will bring: "when the sounds of war will be for ever stilled, the darkness of evil scattered, and all your children gathered into one." Finally, the closing trinitarian petition begins with an exquisitely balanced christological statement: "We ask this through him whose coming is certain, whose day draws near: your Son, our Lord Jesus Christ."

Now let us look at another example in which the 1998 Missal excels. In the light of the readings for Year B (Isa 63:16-17; 64:1, 3-8; 1 Cor 1:3-9; Mark 13:33-37), the priest may use a different opening prayer:

Rend the heavens and come down, O God of all the ages!
Rouse us from sleep, deliver us from our heedless ways,[5]
and form us into a watchful people,
   that,[6] at the advent of your Son, he may find us doing what is
      right,
   mindful of all you command. Grant this through him whose
      coming is certain, whose day draws near: your Son, our Lord
      Jesus Christ.

Once again let me offer four comments. First, "O God of all the ages"
hints at the prophet's address to God, "our Redeemer from of old," just
as Isaiah's "doing what is right" matches the plea that Christ "may
find us doing what is right." But it is the opening line of the prayer
("rend the heavens and come down") that exposes the major link with
Isaiah: "O that you would tear open the heavens and come down!"

Second, Paul's language about "the [final] revealing of our Lord
Jesus Christ," our being "strengthened to the end," and proving "blameless on the day of our Lord" approximates to themes in the opening
prayer. What is called Christ's "revealing," "the end," and "the day of
our Lord" appears in the prayer as his "advent," "coming," and "day."
The faithful people will be, as Paul puts it, "strengthened" and made
"blameless," to the extent that, in the words of the prayer, they allow
God to "deliver" and "form" them, and so become "mindful of all"
that God commands.

Third, the gospel pictures watchful servants staying awake and
waiting for the return of their master. They must not be "found asleep"
when "he comes suddenly." The opening prayer turns this command
into a petition: "rouse us from sleep" and "form us into a watchful
people." In a general way, its address to the "God of all the ages" picks
up what Jesus says more concretely about being awake at all times

---

[5] "Our heedless ways" picks up what Dylan Thomas wrote in his 1948 poem
"Fern Hill": "I ran my heedless ways." He echoed a nineteenth-century hymn,
"Dear Lord and Father of mankind, forgive our foolish ways."

[6] It would be clearer to proclaim if the prayer said "so that." For the same
"defect," see the alternative prayer for Year A of the Third Sunday in Advent and
for Year C of the Third Sunday in Ordinary Time (below).

when "the master" might come: "in the evening, or at midnight, or at cockcrow, or at dawn."

Fourth, before leaving this alternative prayer for Year B, we might note how well it can be proclaimed. The second sentence, for instance, is masterful, with its trilogy of powerful verbs: "rouse us, deliver us, and form us." The "doing what is right" is elegantly explained as "mindful of what you command." Once again we can only admire the exquisite balance embodied in "whose coming is certain, whose day draws near."

Now for a third alternative opening prayer, shaped by the readings for Year C (Jer 33:14-16; 1 Thess 3:12–4:2; Luke 2:25-28, 34-36):

> God our Savior, you utter a word of promise and hope,
> and hasten the day of justice and freedom,
> yet we live in a world forgetful of your word,
> our watchfulness dulled by the cares of life.
> Make us attentive to your word, ready to look on your Son when
>   he comes
> with power and great glory. Make us holy and blameless,
> ready to stand secure when the day of his coming shakes the
>   world with terror.
> We ask this through him whose coming is certain, whose day
>   draws near:
> your Son, our Lord Jesus Christ.

All in all, this alternative prayer for Year C successfully weaves together themes and words from the three verses of Jeremiah. This reading begins with the divine assurance, "the *days* are surely coming, says the Lord, when I will fulfill the promise I made to the house of Israel." This promise is spelled out in the two verses that follow: "In those *days* and at that time I will cause a righteous Branch to spring up for David, and he shall execute justice and righteousness in the land. In those *days* Judah will be saved and Jerusalem will live in safety (emphasis added). And this is the name by which it will be called: 'the Lord is our righteousness.'"

The opening words of the prayer sum up the three verses from Jeremiah by saying: "God our Savior, you utter a word of promise and hope [see Jeremiah on the "promise made" to which the "house of Israel" responded with hope], and hasten the day of justice and freedom [see Jeremiah's "justice and righteousness"]." The prophet's "days" that are coming, repeated twice ("in those days and at that time" and "in those days"), echo three times in the prayer: "the day of justice and freedom," "the day of his coming," and the "day" that draws near. The assurance of the prophet that "Judah will be saved and Jerusalem will live in safety," spelled out in these ten words, is drawn together by addressing "God our Savior." The prophet's emphasis on righteousness ("a righteous Branch," "righteousness in the land," and "the Lord is our righteousness") speaks through the prayer's invoking "the day of justice and freedom" and the plea to be made "holy and blameless."

The second reading for the Second Sunday of Advent in Year C ends with Paul saying: "You know what instructions we gave you through the Lord Jesus." The alternative prayer begins with God "uttering a word of promise and hope," a "word" that the "world" forgets, and then goes on to ask that we may be made "attentive to your word." The apostle's "instructions" are specified as "a word of promise and hope." He prays for the Thessalonians: "may he [God] so strengthen your hearts in *holiness* that you may be *blameless* before our God and Father at the *coming* of our Lord Jesus" (emphasis added). The prayer puts this equivalently: "make us holy and blameless, ready to stand secure" at "the day of his [Jesus'] coming."

The gospel passage is taken from Luke's picture of the final coming of the Son of Man. We can easily match the language used by the prayer with that of Luke. This alternative prayer addresses "God our Savior," while Luke uses an equivalent term for salvation by speaking of "the Son of Man coming" and "*redemption* drawing near."[7] The prayer recognizes that in a "world forgetful" of God's word, "our watchfulness" may be "dulled by the cares of life." This parallels the words of Jesus: "be on guard so that your hearts are not weighed down with . . . the worries of this life . . . be alert at all times." The prayer speaks of the Son who "comes with power and great glory," just as

---

[7] Here is the source of the words used by all the alternative prayers for Advent: "through him whose *coming* is certain, whose day *draws near*" (emphasis added).

the gospel pictures "the Son of Man coming in a cloud with power and great glory." Praying to be "ready to stand secure when the day of his [Christ's] coming shakes the world with terror" harmonizes with the gospel's call to "stand up and raise your heads" when, at the coming of the Son of Man, "people will faint with fear and foreboding of what is coming upon the world." As much as, or even more than, the first two readings, the gospel has helped craft this alternative prayer.

Finally, this prayer reveals a tight and helpful structure that helps it to be proclaimed. The opening sentence features a contrast between positive a-b clauses and negative aa-bb clauses: first, "you utter a word of promise, and hasten the day of justice and freedom," and, then, "we live in a world forgetful of your word, our watchfulness dulled by the cares of life." The second part of the prayer yields a sequence of hearing, seeing, and action: hearing attentively "your word," looking "on your Son when he comes," and standing "secure" at "the day of his coming." The adjective "ready" plays a key role in holding together rhetorically this second part. Being "ready to look on your Son when he comes with power and glory" combines nicely with being "ready to stand secure when the day of his coming shakes the world with terror." The repetition of "make us" also functions to weld into unity this second part: "Make us attentive to your word. . . . Make us holy and blameless."

The Third Sunday of Advent

For the Third Sunday of Advent, the opening prayer in the 1970 *Missale Romanum* went as follows: "Deus, qui conspicis populum tuum nativitatis dominicae festivitatem fideliter exspectare, praesta, quaesumus, ut valeamus ad tantae salutis gaudia pervenire, et ea votis solemnibus alacri semper laetitia celebrare."

The 1973 Missal translates as follows: "Lord God, may we, your people, who look forward to the birthday of Christ, experience the joy of salvation and celebrate that feast with love and thanksgiving." This was to imitate the Latin by putting everything into one sentence; as we shall see, the 1998 Missal breaks the opening prayer into two sentences. Rather than "experience" (1973 Missal), *valeamus* should be translated here as "have the strength to" or be "enabled to" reach a goal: namely, "the joys of so great a salvation." The 1973 translation inserts "love and thanksgiving," whereas the original Latin prayer expresses rather the feelings of joy and gladness (*gaudia* and *laetitia*). This translation sets aside the joyful emotions that belong to the Third Sunday of Advent, "Gaudete" Sunday.

The 1998 Missal comes up with this splendid rendering: "Gracious God, your people look forward in hope to the festival of our Savior's birth. Give us the strength to reach that happy day of salvation and to celebrate it with hearts full of joy. We ask this through our Lord Jesus Christ." The translation is felicitous. "Gracious God" catches the implication of the verb in *Deus, qui conspicis*. God does not merely "see" his people but looks upon them with kindness. Then, a strictly literal translation should tell of "looking forward in *faith* to the festival of *the Lord's* birth." But looking forward is a matter of hope; likewise the *votis* of the last line of the Latin text should probably be understood as "hopes" or "desires," rather than "prayers." Hence the 1998 Missal proposes "look forward in hope." Another happy touch is the use of "our [rather than 'the'] Savior," reinforcing the personal sense already conveyed by "your people." Similarly, the emphasis on *tantae salutis* and celebration encourages naming Jesus as the "Savior" rather than as the "Lord" (from *dominicae*) who will be born. Lastly, "that happy day of salvation" captures well the sense of *tantae salutis gaudia*. Finally, "to celebrate it with hearts full of joy" draws together *votis solemnibus alacri semper laetitia celebrare*. It combines in a note of "fullness" the "always" (*semper*) and "eager" (*alacri*) of the Latin text. Celebrating "with hearts full of joy" uncovers the meaning of celebrating with *votis solemnibus* (traditional desires/hopes) the birth of Christ.

One should also add that this translation is easy to proclaim. It begins with a statement about God's people "looking forward in hope" to the birth of Christ. Then it turns to ask for "the strength *to reach* that happy day of salvation and *to celebrate* it with hearts full of joy" (emphasis added). A neat balance is achieved between reaching and celebrating.

The word-for-word method of the 2010 Missal supplies the translation: "O God, who see [!][8] how your people faithfully await the feast

---

[8] It would be correct English to write, "who sees"; it would be better English to write, "you see."

of the Lord's Nativity, enable us, we pray, to attain the joys of so great a salvation and to celebrate them [!] always with solemn worship and glad rejoicing. Through our Lord Jesus Christ." A series of failings mar this version. It gets off to an awkward start, with "O God, who see." As I pointed out in chapter 3, "O God, who" as a form of address belongs to classical Latin and not to contemporary English. "See" neglects the personal implications of *conspicis*, with its hint of kindly involvement in what is seen. This translation proceeds to capitalize "nativity," even though the original Latin is not capitalized, and to choose a "sacral" word ("Nativity") over the straightforward "birth." In this version it would have made better English to move the *quaesumus* (we pray) to the end and complete the collect with a grammatical period: "We ask this through . . ." Worst of all, dogged attention to the Latin has produced the false, self-regarding suggestion that at Christmas we celebrate *our own joys*! "Them" refers to an earlier plural noun, and the closest plural noun that precedes is "joys." But surely what we celebrate is not our own joys but the birth of Christ (what the 1998 translation calls "that happy day of salvation" to which "it" refers back). The one breathless sentence of this translation leaves it far behind the 1998 translation. Please read out loud the two versions and you should agree.

Let us take up now the alternative opening prayers for the Third Sunday in Advent that the 1998 Missal provides for Years A, B, and C. The readings for Year A are as follows: Isaiah 35:1-6, 10; James 5:7-10; Matthew 11:2-11. These readings are introduced in the 1998 Missal by this opening prayer:

> God of *glory* and compassion, at your touch the *wilderness blossoms*,
> broken lives are made whole, and *fearful hearts* grow *strong* in faith.
> Open our eyes to your presence and awaken our hearts to sing your praise.
> To all who long for your Son's return grant perseverance and patience,
> that we may announce in word and deed the good news of the kingdom.

First, the words in the added italics are taken directly from Isaiah's language about "the glory of the Lord" and "the wilderness" that "shall blossom," and his message: "Say to those who are of fearful heart, be strong." What the prayer says about "broken lives" being "made whole" summarizes not only Isaiah's promise of healing for the blind, the deaf, the lame, and the dumb but also the joy and gladness that will come to those who are weary and afraid. At the beginning and at the end, the reading from the prophet focuses on "joy." Even if the prayer does not explicitly include the word "joy," its mood is that of a fresh joy that "sings the praise" of God.

Second, we should not miss how the "patience" requested by the prayer permeates the passage from James. He instructs his readers to expect "the coming of the Lord" like "patient" farmers waiting for their crops (three times) and so imitate the "patience" of the prophets.

Third, the gospel reading returns to themes of Isaiah: "the wilderness" (where John the Baptist preached) and the healing of broken lives (in the ministry of Jesus). Its reference to "the good news being proclaimed to the poor" supplies the background for the plea "to announce in word and deed the good news of the kingdom." The last line of the gospel refers expressly to "the kingdom of heaven."

Fourth, this first alternative prayer follows the traditional four-part pattern of collects by *addressing* God ("God of glory and compassion") and providing a *motivating* clause ("at your touch . . . strong in faith"). Then comes a *petition* ("Open our eyes . . . praise") and a *purpose* (so "that we may announce . . . the good news of the kingdom").[9] Vivid language characterizes this prayer, not least in the motivating clause: "at your touch the wilderness blossoms, broken lives are made whole, and fearful hearts grow strong in faith."

The petition opens with a neat balance between its two clauses: "Open our eyes to your presence and awaken our hearts to sing your praise." The sequence of "presence" and "praise," followed at once by "perseverance" and "patience," provides a pleasing alliteration. With its four central sentences, along with the concluding "We ask

---

[9] See Moore, *Vatican II and the Collects for Ordinary Time*, 13–15.

this through him whose coming is certain, whose day draws near: your Son," the first alternative prayer displays rich qualities for an Advent collect.

Let us now examine how the second alternative prayer has been shaped by the readings of Year B: Isaiah 61:1-2, 10-11; 1 Thessalonians 5:16-24; John 1:6-8, 19-28.

> O God, most high and most near, you send glad tidings to the
> *lowly*,
> you hide not your face from the *poor*; those who dwell in dark-
> ness you call into the light.
> Take away our blindness, remove the hardness of our hearts,
> and form us into a *humble* people,
> that, at the advent of your Son, we may recognize him in our
> midst
> and find joy in his saving presence. (emphasis added)

The adjectives "lowly," "poor," and "humble" resonate with the opening verse from Isaiah and its picture of "bringing the good news to the humble/poor." "Finding joy in his [the Son's] saving presence" converges with the sentiments of the prophet: "I will greatly rejoice in the Lord." Calling God "most high and most near" sums up the prophetic image of God as being both exalted "Lord" and tenderly close to his people.

The opening words from Paul, "Rejoice always," also stand behind the prayer to "find joy in his saving presence." The apostle pleads: "May the God of peace himself sanctify you entirely, and may your spirit, soul, and body be kept sound and blameless." The language is different, but the vision of total healing and sanctifying is reflected in the prayer about being "called to the light," being delivered from "blindness" and "hardness of heart," and "formed into a humble people."

The gospel begins by invoking three times "the light" to which John the Baptist testifies. The prayer takes up the binary contrasts of light/darkness and the associated "blindness," caused by "the hardness of our hearts." John speaks also of one "standing among you whom you do not know," which prompts the plea "to recognize him in our midst."

Like the other prayers, this alternative prayer reads very well and is structured to be proclaimed easily and intelligibly. The faithful can readily understand what is being said and are in a position to respond with their "Amen." Saint Augustine of North Africa pictures this situation as his "blessing and invoking" God, "so that as the sounds break from our mouth and make themselves heard, the populace may answer 'Amen'" (*Confessions*, 13.34).[10]

The triple shape of the *motivating* sentence is effective: "you send glad tidings to the lowly, you hide not your face from the poor; those who dwell in darkness you call into the light." The threefold shape of the *petition* is at least as effective: "Take away our blindness, remove the hardness of our hearts, and form us into a humble people." The prayer clearly states its *purpose*: "that, at the advent of your Son, we may recognize him in our midst and find joy in his saving presence."

A third alternative prayer follows the readings for Year C: Zephaniah 3:14-18; Philippians 4:4-7; and Luke 3:10-18.

> Almighty God, you sent your Son into a world
> where the wheat must be winnowed from the chaff
> and evil clings even to what is good.
> Let the fire of your Spirit purge us of greed and deceit,
> so that, purified, we may find our peace in you and you may
> delight in us.

We can take up the prayer, phrase by phrase, and see where it aligns itself with the language of the scriptural readings. Luke announces the One who is coming: "his winnowing fork in his hand to clear his threshing floor and to gather the wheat into his granary, but the

---

[10] *The Confessions*, trans. Maria Boulding (Hyde Park, NY: New City Press, 1997), 367. In *De catechizandis rudibus* (chap. 7), Augustine insists that problems with language should be corrected "so that the people might say Amen to what they plainly understand." In sermon 293.3, he vividly describes such good communication: "as I wish to speak to you, I look for a way of how what is already in my mind may also be found in yours" (*Sermon* 293.3, in Augustine, *Sermons*, The Works of Saint Augustine: A Translation for the 21st Century, Vol. III, no. 8, *Sermons 273–305A*, trans. Edmund Hill, OP [Hyde Park, NY: New City Press, 1994], 150). Over and over again, the alternative prayers provide such means for readily communicating to the assembled faithful what is, presumably, already in the heart and mind of the presiding minister.

chaff he will burn with unquenchable fire." The Missal transposes this image into the motivation: "you sent your Son into a world where the wheat must be winnowed from the chaff and evil clings even to what is good."

The gospel reports how John exhorted tax collectors and soldiers, respectively, to "collect only the amount prescribed" and "to be satisfied with" their "wages." Like us, through "the fire of the Spirit," they were to be "purged" of "greed and deceit."

In a similar way, "finding peace" in God represents Paul's guarantee: "the peace of God which surpasses all understanding will guard your hearts and your minds in Christ Jesus." "That God may delight in us" looks back to Zephaniah's promise: "The Lord, your God . . . will rejoice over you with gladness; he will renew you in his love."

I hope to have deepened the reader's appreciation of what the 1998 Missal did for the opening prayers of two Sundays in Advent, both its translations of the collects in the 1970 *Missale Romanum* and its original compositions, the three alternative prayers shaped by the readings for Sundays in Years A, B, and C, respectively.

Let us move to the opening prayers of the Third and Fourth Sundays of Ordinary Time. We begin with the 1998 Missal's translation of the collect in the 1970 *Missale Romanum*.

The Third Sunday of Ordinary Time

The Latin text for the Third Sunday of Ordinary Time goes as follows: "Omnipotens sempiterne Deus, dirige actus nostros in beneplacito tuo, ut in nomine dilecti Filii tui mereamur bonis operibus abundare."[11] The 1998 Missal offers this translation: "Almighty and eternal God, direct *all* our actions to accord with your *holy* will, that *our lives* may be rich in good works *done* in the name of your beloved Son" (emphasis added).

By inserting the words I have indicated in italics but without altering the meaning, this version of the opening prayer makes a cryptic

---

[11] On this collect, see Moore, *Vatican II and The Collects for Ordinary Time*, 444–56.

Latin prayer more immediately intelligible to those who hear it proclaimed. The parallelism between "all our actions" and "our lives" holds together the two clauses. So too does the parallelism between "to accord with your holy will" and "may be rich in good works done in the name of your beloved Son," with "your holy will" being echoed by "your beloved Son." Translating *mereamur bonis operibus abundare* as "may be rich in good works" is masterly, from the point of good English and good theology. It would be quite misleading to translate: "may merit to abound in good works."[12] In some secondary sense (but only in some secondary sense),[13] the *prior good works* of human beings have the result of meriting a reward. But *prior merit* does not cause good works to abound. Merits result from good works; they do not "cause" them.

As with other seasons of the liturgical year, the 1998 Missal provides alternative opening prayers that correspond to the scriptural readings assigned for Years A, B, and C. For the Third Sunday of Year A in Ordinary Time, the readings are: Isaiah 8:23–9:3; 1 Corinthians 1:10-13, 17; Matthew 4:12-23.

For this Sunday, we have the alternative collect:

> God of salvation, the splendor of your glory dispels the darkness
>   of earth,
> for in Christ we behold the nearness of your kingdom.
> Now make us quick to follow where he beckons, eager to embrace
>   the tasks of the gospel. We ask this through our Lord Jesus
>   Christ, your Son.

When we unravel the biblical sources, the first line of the prayer picks up the promise from Isaiah that God will "make glorious the way of the sea." In fact, "the people who walked in darkness have seen a great light; those who lived in a land of deep darkness—on them light has shined."

---

[12] Even the 2010 Missal refrains from such a rendering and translates the clause as "we may abound in good works."

[13] Remember the principle from St. Augustine cited in chapter 3 above: when God crowns our merits, he does nothing else but crown the divine gifts.

Matthew quotes these words and more from Isaiah as being fulfilled in Jesus, who "began proclaiming, 'the kingdom of heaven is near.'" In terms of the collect, "for in Christ we behold the nearness of the kingdom." That motivates the confession that "the splendor" of the divine glory "dispels the darkness of earth." The gospel presses on to describe the call of Simon Peter, Andrew, James, and John. By instantly dropping their work as fishermen and following Jesus, they depict what the collect asks for: "Make us quick to follow where he [Christ] beckons, eager to embrace the tasks of the gospel." Thus the first reading and Matthew's gospel have yielded much for the making of the prayer. Only one theme links the second reading to the prayer. Paul's mission to "proclaim the gospel" implies the good news of the kingdom that Jesus proclaimed (and personified) and for which he called the four apostles. The prayer ends by asking for eagerness "to embrace the tasks of the gospel."

Unobtrusively this alternative collect creates a neat, "logical" sequence. Since the divine glory has dispelled the darkness of our earthly home, we are now enabled to "behold" in Christ the nearness of God's kingdom. We can also be "made quick" to follow his call, because we now see him "beckoning" to us.

The Third Sunday of Ordinary Time in Year B prescribes as readings: Jonah 3:1-5, 10; 1 Corinthians 7:29-31; and Mark 1:14-20. For this Sunday the 1998 Missal offers the following alternative opening prayer:

> Your sovereign rule, O Lord, draws near to us in the person of Jesus your Son. Your word summons us to faith, your power transforms our lives.
> Free us to follow in Christ's footsteps, so that neither human loyalty nor earthly attachment may hold us back from answering your call.
> We ask this through our Lord Jesus Christ.

Five comments suggest themselves. First, the people of Nineveh believed in God and renounced their evil behavior when the "sovereign rule of God drew near to them in the person" of the prophet Jonah. In that sense, the first reading has helped inspire the collect. But Paul and Mark's gospel have provided more for the prayer.

Second, Paul's message about the appointed time that has grown short and a world that is passing away prompts him into urging the Corinthian Christians to be detached not only from their possessions and worldly engagements but even from their married and familial commitments and experiences. In the language of the alternative prayer, "human loyalty" and "earthly attachment" should not "hold them back from answering" God's call that comes through Christ.

Third, the passage from Mark's gospel opens by announcing that "Jesus came proclaiming the good news of God and saying, 'the time is fulfilled and the kingdom of God has come near; repent and believe in the good news.'" The prayer, in effect, paraphrases this: "Your sovereign rule, O God, draws near to us in the person of Jesus your Son. Your Word summons us to faith, your power transforms our lives." Here the prayer sometimes uses closely matching expressions: for instance, "sovereign rule" for "kingdom of God," "draws near" for "has come near," and "summoned to faith" for "believe in the good news."

The gospel passage turns personal and particular when it recounts the call of Peter, Andrew, James, and John. At once they leave their nets and their families to become "fishers for human beings." Their story exemplifies what the prayer asks for: "free us to follow in Christ's footsteps, so that neither human loyalty nor earthly attachment may hold us back from answering your call."

Fourth, once again an alternative prayer displays the classical four-part structure of the traditional collects. An *address* to God as "sovereign ruler" introduces a *motivating* statement: "your rule draws near to us in the person of Jesus your Son. Your word summons us to faith, your power transforms our lives." This provides the setting for a *petition*: "Free us to follow in Christ's footsteps." The *purpose* completes the prayer: "so that neither human loyalty nor earthly attachment may hold us back from answering your call."

Fifth and finally, there is much to admire in the structure and language of the prayer, not least the effectively balanced exposition of what happens when God's "rule" "draws near to us in the person of Jesus": "Your word summons us to faith, your power transforms our lives." In a spare and nuanced fashion, the clauses describe the two inseparable aspects of what the divine kingdom brings: revelation (the "word" that "summons us to faith") and salvation (the "power" that "transforms our lives"). This sets together the revelatory Word of John's gospel with Paul's sense of the gospel as being the "power of God for salvation" (Rom 1:16).[14]

The readings for Year C of the Third Sunday in Ordinary Time are as follows: Nehemiah 8:2-6, 8-10; 1 Corinthians 12:12-30; and Luke 1:1-4; 4:14-21. This is the alternative prayer provided by the 1998 Missal:

> Lord God, whose compassion embraces all peoples,
> whose law is wisdom, freedom, and joy for the poor,
> fulfil in our midst your promise of favor, that we may receive
>   the gospel of salvation with faith and, anointed by the Spirit,
>   freely proclaim it.[15]

The first reading tells how Ezra, priest and scribe, read to the people the Law of the Lord (with the "Law" mentioned at the start of passage, at the halfway mark, and at the end).[16] Ezra assured the people that the Torah is truly a source of joy: "the joy of the Lord is your strength." The prayer obviously follows suit, with its words about the "law" being "wisdom, freedom, and joy."

Apropos of Paul's elaborate reflection on the variety of gifts and functions that Christians have received, the prayer is more elusive in taking up themes. We might refer what is said about the divine "com-

---

[14] Judgments differ, but I consider the "so that" which leads from the petition ("Free us to follow in Christ's footsteps") to the purpose ("so that neither human loyalty") better English than the mere "that" often used by the 1998 Missal to make such a connection. "So that" also makes the transition a little clearer when proclaimed.

[15] In my judgment, the prayer could be improved by substituting "your" for "whose": "Lord God, your compassion embraces all peoples, your law. . . ."

[16] This first reading stresses how Ezra enabled the people to hear "with understanding" what he was reading (Neh 8:2, 3, 8). This suggests the difference between the 1998 Missal (as consistently and immediately understandable) and the 2010 Missal (at times obscure and even unintelligible). The gospel for this Sunday reports Jesus himself reading (not to the whole people but those gathered in the synagogue at Nazareth) a brief passage from Isaiah (rather than long sections from the Torah). But, like Ezra, Jesus interpreted what he had read, so that those present could understand.

passion embracing *all* peoples" to the apostle's opening reminder: "in the one Spirit we were *all* baptized into one body—Jews or Greeks, slaves or free—and we were *all* made to drink of one Spirit."

We should have little difficulty in spotting parallels between the passage from Luke and the proposed alternative prayer. Jesus reads from Isaiah: "*The Spirit of the Lord* is upon me, because he has *anointed* me to bring *good news* [*gospel*] *to the poor.* He has sent me to *proclaim* release to the captives and recovery of sight to the blind, to let the oppressed go *free,* to *proclaim* the year of *the Lord's favor.*" Jesus then sits down and says: "Today this scripture [which is a *promise*] has been *fulfilled* in your hearing." This passage, as indicated by the italics, supplies the vocabulary for the prayer motivated by the confession that God's law is "*freedom and joy for the poor*": "*fulfill* in our midst your *promise* of *favor,* that we may receive the *gospel* of salvation with faith, and *anointed by the Spirit, freely proclaim* it." Where Jesus speaks of a promise "fulfilled in your hearing," the prayer follows suit by asking: "fulfill in our midst your promise of favor." The biblical language about bringing good news to the poor, releasing captives, giving sight to the blind, and liberating the oppressed is summed up as "the gospel of salvation." It can also be described as divine "compassion," a word with which the prayer opens.

All in all, this alternative collect proves itself profoundly scriptural in its inspiration. It also sets the bar very high for Christians. Where Jesus had been anointed by the Holy Spirit to proclaim the good news, now they are reminded of their anointing by the Spirit, which should enable them to "freely proclaim" the same good news.

The Fourth Sunday of Ordinary Time

The Latin text for the opening prayer of the Fourth Sunday in Ordinary Time is as follows: "Concede nobis, Dominus Deus noster, ut te tota mente veneremur, et omnes homines rationabili diligamus affectu."[17] The 1998 Missal translated this succinct, even laconic,

---

[17] On this collect, see Moore, *Vatican II and the Collects for Ordinary Time,* 99–115.

collect: "Teach us, Lord God, to worship you with undivided hearts and to cherish all people with true and faithful love."

The "two interconnected petitions"[18] that make up this prayer evoke the episode in Matthew 22:37-40 in which Jesus joined together the Old Testament commands to love God (Deut 6:4-6) and love one's neighbor (Lev 19:18). By replacing "love" of God with "worship," the prayer offers a pointed reminder that worship should express our love of God and implies loving God totally. The loving worship of God and a "sincere and active love towards all others" belong inseparably together.[19] The love of God expressed in worship results in authentic love toward all other people. Translating *rationabili* as "true and faithful" should not distract us. As used in ancient ecclesiastical Latin, this adjective might be translated as "spiritual," but "true and faithful" profiles what such love means.[20]

As usual, the 1998 Missal offers alternative opening prayers that focus on themes in the prescribed readings. These are, for Year A, Zephaniah 2:3; 3:12-13; 1 Corinthians 1:26-31; and Matthew 5:1-12. For this Sunday we have the following collect:

> O God, teach us the hidden wisdom of the gospel,
> so that we may hunger and thirst for holiness,
> work tirelessly for peace,
> and be counted among those
> who seek first the blessedness of your kingdom.

When God grants the petition ("teach us the wisdom of the gospel"), it can have three striking and memorable results. We will "hunger and thirst for holiness," "work tirelessly for peace," and "be counted among those who seek first the blessedness of your kingdom."

The petition speaks immediately of Christ the mysterious "wisdom of God," celebrated by Paul in the second reading. The three results invite the congregation to listen attentively to the beatitudes presented in the passage from the Gospel of Matthew. The prayer ("that we may hunger and thirst for holiness") develops significantly the beatitude

---

[18] Ibid., 102.
[19] Ibid., 112.
[20] Ibid., 108–12.

that applies to "those who hunger and thirst for righteousness." Paul has called Christ "our righteousness and our *holiness*." In hungering and thirsting for righteousness, we are seeking Christ who is in person "our righteousness and our holiness." "Work tirelessly for peace" matches the beatitude for "the peacemakers." "Seeking first the blessedness of your kingdom" draws not only on the language of "blessedness" found in all the beatitudes but also on the double reference to God's "kingdom" (Matt 5:3, 10). "Seeking first" comes from a later passage in the same Sermon on the Mount: "seek first the kingdom and its righteousness" (Matt 6:33). Thus this alternative opening prayer invites the worshipers to think of the beatitudes not in an isolated fashion but within the whole context of the Sermon on the Mount. Being *"counted* among those who seek first the blessedness of your kingdom" echoes the use of "counted" in such biblical passages as Acts 5:41. There "the apostles rejoiced because they were counted worthy to suffer dishonor for the sake of the name [of Jesus]."

Thus this alternative collect for the Fourth Sunday of Ordinary Time in Year A holds firmly to the second reading and the gospel passage. What then about the first reading? We should not miss ways in which the reading from Zephaniah about a humble and lowly people foreshadows what Jesus says in the beatitudes about "the poor in spirit" and "the meek."

The readings for Year B of the Fourth Sunday in Ordinary Time are: Deuteronomy 18:15-20; 1 Corinthians 7:32-35; and Mark 1:21-28. The following alternative opening prayer is proposed:

> Faithful *God*, your *Holy One, Jesus of Nazareth*,
> spoke the truth with *authority*,
> and you confirmed his *teaching* by wondrous [why not wonderful?] deeds.
> Through his healing presence, drive far from us all that is unholy,
> so that by word and deed we may proclaim him Messiah and Lord
> and bear witness to your power to heal and save. (emphasis added)

In a satisfying way, this alternative prayer exemplifies the *traditional, four-part pattern* of collects. First, it *addresses* God ("Faithful God"); then it moves to a *motivating* clause: "your Holy One, Jesus of Nazareth, spoke the word with authority, and you confirmed his teaching by wondrous deeds." Then comes a *petition*: "through his healing presence, drive far from us all that is unholy." Finally, the *purpose* takes a balanced, double form: "so that [a] by word and deed we may proclaim him Messiah and Lord, and [b] bear witness to your power to heal and save." Three pairs of words heighten the rhetorical effectiveness of the purpose: "word and deed," "Messiah and Lord," and "heal and save." Stylistically, the prayer is satisfying. What of its theology?

From a *theological point of view*, the prayer blends revelation (word) and salvation (deed)—coming primarily through the mediation of Jesus himself. As Revealer, he "spoke the truth with authority" and engaged in "teaching." As Savior, he performed "wondrous deeds," embodies a "healing presence," can "drive away from us all that is unholy," and enjoys the divine "power to heal and save." Then "we" also have a revelatory function, albeit a subordinate one: "by word and deed we may proclaim him Messiah and Lord and bear witness to your power to heal and save." Revelation is also communicated through what we "proclaim" and "bear witness to."

The prescribed gospel from Mark, which centers on the deliverance of a man with an unclean spirit, deeply shapes this alternative collect. He is healed and saved. The italicized words in the first line of the collect (see above) derive directly from what the unclean spirit says: "What have you to do with us, *Jesus of Nazareth*? Have you come to destroy us? I know who you are, the *Holy One of God.*" The gospel twice speaks of the "teaching" and "authority" of Jesus (Mark 1:22, 27), both of which feature firmly in the motivating clause of the collect. The gospel passage also speaks three times of "unclean" spirit(s). Instead of asking, however, that God "drive far from us all that is unclean," the prayer suggests what is opposed to "your Holy One" by speaking of "all that is unholy," which Christ's "healing presence" will "drive far from us."

Even if they attract less attention, the *first two readings* enjoy links with the alternative collect. The passage from Deuteronomy about God's promise to raise up a prophet like Moses and put words into his mouth justifies not only the address of "Faithful God" but also what is said about the prophetic role of Jesus, who "spoke the truth with authority." The Deuteronomy passage also serves as a proper background to what the prayer says about "speaking the truth with authority," "teaching," "word," "proclaiming," and "bearing witness." Then, proclaiming Jesus as "Lord" finds its counterpart in the second reading when Paul twice cites "the Lord" and twice "the Lord's affairs."

Year C prescribes these readings for the Fourth Sunday of Ordinary Time: Jeremiah 1:4-5, 17-19; 1 Corinthians 12:31–13:13; Luke 4:21-30. The alternative opening prayer goes as follows:

> God of salvation, in your Prophet, Jesus the Christ,
> you announce freedom and summon us to conversion.
> As we marvel at the grace and power of your word,
> enlighten us to see the beauty of the gospel
> and strengthen us to embrace its demands.

This collect has created a pleasing structure, with balancing phrases and clauses that begin with "God of salvation" and "your Prophet, Jesus the Christ." Then "you announce freedom" is twinned with "summon us to conversion" and "the grace" is twinned with the "power of the word." The prayer ends with a petition that involves revelation in effective counterpoint with a petition that involves salvation: "*enlighten* us to *see* the beauty of the gospel and *strengthen* us to embrace its demands." The collect serves very well for proclamation, since it focuses and holds the attention of the congregation.

All in all, the links with the readings come across as less emphatic than in the other alternative prayers we have examined. "God of salvation" calls forth the central topic of the Gospel of Luke appointed for Year C: from the start, Luke highlights the saving work of God (e.g. 1:47, 69, 71, 77; 2:17, 30). Jesus as Prophet reflects the prophetic calling of Jeremiah, the theme of this Sunday's first reading. "Announcing freedom" and "summoning to conversion" constitute the heart of the passage that leads into the opening verses of today's gospel. Initially the people were "amazed at the gracious words that came from his [Jesus'] mouth"— a reaction transposed into "we marvel at the grace and power of your word." But they attempted to murder Jesus, instead of being "enlightened to see the beauty of the gospel and strengthened to embrace its demands." Their tragic failure stands over against the lovely message Jesus offered. The beauty of the gospel, along with its demands, also shines through the second reading, Paul's wonderful and vital hymn to love.

Conclusions

This chapter has examined sixteen collects found in the 1998 Missal for two Sundays of Advent and two Sundays of Ordinary Time—four translations of collects from the (Latin) 1970 Missal and twelve new collects prepared expressly for the 1998 Missal. Whether in the translated texts or in the new ones, the 1998 Missal towers over the "halfway," word-for-word "English" of the 2010 Missal. This chapter found that the 1998 translation of the Latin collects was consistently closer to the meaning of the original and avoided the theological error found in the 2010 Missal's rendering of the collect for the First Sunday of Advent. The alternative opening prayers provided by the 1998 Missal draw expertly on the scriptural readings, prove theologically insightful, and, through their first-rate English, can be effectively proclaimed at the liturgical assembly. Browsing through them is reading one good thing after another.

Gerard Moore, an Australian liturgist on whom I have drawn, has published a scholarly and well-judged commentary on the collects for Sundays in Ordinary Time in the 1973 Missal. We would be blessed if other specialists did the same for the alternative opening prayers contained in the 1998 Missal. Thanks to the Canterbury Press's publication of *Opening Prayers* in 1999, these alternative collects are widely available. While officially sidelined, they remain gloriously successful—landmark compositions in the history of English-speaking liturgy.

A Coda: Bruce Harbert's Criticism of the 1998 Collects

In an article published in 1996, when the texts of the 1998 Missal were already available, Bruce Harbert sniffed out "a propensity towards Pelagianism" found in some of its collects.[21] In view of the fact

---

[21] Bruce Harbert, "What Kind of Missal are we Getting?" *New Blackfriars* 77 (1996): 548–52, at 551.

that he was to become in 2002 the executive director of the secretariat of the new ICEL, there was an unconscious irony in this criticism that would be revealed in the 2010 Missal. That translation, as we have repeatedly seen, indulges a clearly Pelagian theology. It was a translation developed on Harbert's watch.

He detected a Pelagian tendency in the translation provided by the collects of the 1998 Missal—he called it ICEL 2—for the Twenty-Fourth and Twenty-Fifth Sundays in Ordinary Time. The first of these "Pelagian" collects goes as follows: "O God, Creator and Ruler of all that is, look kindly upon the prayers of your servants: grant that we may serve you with undivided hearts and so experience the power of your mercy." Harbert complained that "and so" gives "the impression that God's response to our efforts is automatic."[22] He misread the text. It is not a matter of "God's response to our efforts," but rather God's further action ("the power" of divine mercy) that we will experience after the divine grace that has first made it possible for us to serve God "with undivided hearts." The 1998 collect envisages two actions of God that we genuinely pray for; we do not automatically take for granted the second of these two actions (God's powerful mercy that we experience).

The collect for the Twenty-Fifth Sunday in Ordinary Time of the 1998 Missal prays: "Lord our God, upon the two commandments to love you and love our neighbor you have founded all your holy law. Give us the grace to keep these commandments and so inherit ['inherit,' not 'merit'] eternal life." Once again Harbert detected a Pelagian tendency in the "and so"; the two words give the impression that "God's response to our efforts is automatic."[23] But the collect is not indicating a divine response, automatic or otherwise, but rather a happy result ("inheriting eternal life") that will follow on God first giving us the grace to keep the two foundational commandments of love.

If there is Pelagianism to be detected, it comes rather in the 2010 Missal that Harbert helped to prepare. For the same Twenty-Fifth Sunday in Ordinary Time, its collect expects us to pray: "O God, who founded all the commands of your sacred Law upon love of you and

---

[22] Ibid., 551.
[23] Ibid.

of our neighbor, grant that, by keeping your precepts, *we may merit to attain eternal life*" (emphasis added). This sounds like a Pelagian, do-it-yourself salvation.

In his hunt for Pelagian tendencies, Harbert named also the 1998 translation of the collect for the Twenty-Sixth Sunday in Ordinary Time and quoted it: "that we may strive for the things you have promised and come to share the treasures of heaven." He convicted these words of the opening prayer of giving less than appropriate space for "the divine initiative."[24] He could pass that judgment since he had remained silent about the words that came before: "let your grace descend upon us without ceasing." Such an unceasing input of grace can make it possible to strive for the things God has promised.

In dismissing the 1998 Missal's translation of the collect for the Eleventh Sunday in Ordinary Time as "a more striking example of Pelagianism," Harbert cited it as saying "without you we are weak and certain to fall," but *omitted* significant words that followed: "grant us always the help of your grace, that in following your commands we may please you in desire and deed." How anyone could find striking Pelagianism in a prayer that confesses that we "always" need the help of God's grace (in both our desires and our deeds) eludes me.

Harbert was clearly very cross with the opening prayers of the 1998 Missal. In a further example, he argued, on the basis of one little word, that the collect for the Sixth Sunday in Ordinary Time "*erases the whole notion* of God dwelling in the human heart by grace" (emphasis added), a precious concept developed initially by the Eastern Fathers.[25] This dreadful "erasing" came about because the collect spoke, not of God remaining "in," but only of "remaining *with* those whose hearts are faithful and just" (emphasis added).[26] Once again Harbert failed to quote the whole text: "O God, you promise to remain with those whose

---

[24] Ibid.

[25] Ibid., 552.

[26] The Latin for this 1970 collect was drawn from an ancient source and runs as follows: "Deus, qui te in rectis et sinceris manere pectoribus asseris, da nobis tua gratia tales exsistere, in quibus habitare digneris." For the origin and meaning of the prayer, see Moore, *Vatican II and the Collects for Ordinary Time*, 323–37.

hearts are faithful and just. By the gift of your grace make our lives worthy of your abiding presence." The "abiding presence" of God with "hearts" that are faithful and just can suggest to an attentive reader echoes of Jesus' words about "abiding" in his love (John 15:9).

Gerard Moore illustrates the post-Ascension thrust of the collect in question. Instead of being primarily concerned with what Harbert calls "God dwelling in the human heart [singular] by grace" (which focuses on the individual), this prayer asks rather for "God's ever-abiding presence in the Christian community on earth." Christ is now enthroned in heaven and "the faithful request the gift of such hearts that they may be the sort of community in which God dwells."[27]

When Cardinal Medina (a Chilean) and his secretary, Archbishop Francesco Pio Tamburrino (an Italian), peremptorily rejected the English translation of the 1998 Missal, presumably they were influenced by certain English-speaking advisors. Was Harbert already involved at that stage, even before he became an official of the new ICEL? If so, some of the advice he was giving was inaccurate and unconvincing—to judge from the unhappy article he published in 1996.

---

[27] Ibid., 324, 326.

Chapter Six

A Tale of Two Missals (1998 and 2010)

Sixteen years of work (1982–98) on the 1998 Missal were swept aside when Cardinal Medina summarily dismissed this translation, which had been prepared by the original ICEL and approved by all the English-speaking conferences of bishops, and moved to create a new ICEL, now firmly under Vatican control. In *It's the Eucharist, Thank God*, Bishop Taylor tells the story of that scandalous takeover. Originally established by the bishops' conferences and responsible to them, ICEL was transformed into a branch of the Congregation for Divine Worship and the Discipline of the Sacraments. The A team of the original ICEL was replaced by a B team, which went on to produce a new translation amid more scandalous circumstances. As we saw in chapter 3, *after* the conferences of English-speaking bishops had reluctantly accepted this new translation, thousands of changes were unilaterally introduced. Even by Vatican standards, this was a remarkable assertion of central authority (or should we say power?) and disrespect for the responsible, collegial function of bishops with and under Peter.

Let us now sum up what the faithful of the Roman Rite lost and what they have been saddled with. They lost the 1998 Missal and were burdened with the 2010 Missal.

The 1998 Missal

Rather than sounding like stiff and awkward "translation" English, the 1998 Missal is eminently suitable for proclamation. Its language proves natural and clearly understandable, both for those who proclaim the texts and those who hear them. The prayers have been translated to be proclaimed *and heard.* During the liturgical celebration itself, the faithful do not need to check the written texts in order to understand what they are listening to. The oral communication of the 1998 Missal will be effective, provided the celebrants speak up, enunciate clearly the words, and project their voices.

The translators of the 1998 Missal also took to heart the warnings of the instruction *Comme le prévoit* against using "so-called sacral vocabulary" (CLP 17) and language that is pompous and superfluous (CLP 34). As we illustrated in the last chapter, the opening prayers consistently display a pleasing, contemporary rhythm and cadence. Throughout they are marked by good English vocabulary and expression.

Vatican II's Constitution on the Sacred Liturgy prescribed proper, organic development in the new forms to be introduced (SC 23). The ancient Roman Rite, as the experts who prepared the constitution knew very well, had not been frozen in time. *Comme le prévoit* recognized that the "creation" of new texts was not only licit but even necessary (CLP 43). The 1998 Missal did just that—in particular, with its alternative opening prayers.

Composed with clear reference to the scriptural readings, these new prayers support a harmonious, thematic unity within the liturgy. Moreover, since many Christians read and hear the same readings on Sunday, the alternative opening prayers help to promote ecumenical unity. The prayers help them to be united at the table of the Word of the Lord, even if they are not yet united at the table of the Lord's Body and Blood. Here as elsewhere, as an instruction for the translators, *Comme le prévoit* encouraged valuable outcomes.

The 2010 Missal

As far as I know, the overwhelming case Peter Jeffery brought against *Liturgiam Authenticam,* the unfortunate instruction that the Vatican imposed in place of *Comme le prévoit,* has never been properly answered. The unsatisfactory principles for translation set out in *Liturgiam Authenticam* stood squarely behind the deficiencies of the 2010 Missal.

That translation, in a quest for a mythical "sacred vernacular," favors odd, "stately" words, obsequious ways of addressing God, and a non-inclusive language that leaves out half the human race. Lacking all ecumenical sensibility, it mistranslates the creeds. All too often its translations are misleading and even theologically false (for example, a Pelagian tendency shows up now and then). Over and over again, the 2010 Missal is hard to proclaim—not least because of its long, Latin sentences that do not fit the English language. Its literalist, word-for-word translation becomes even odder when it insists on capitalizing words that even the Latin original leaves in lower case. Is the celebrating priest meant to indicate the presence of capitals by pronouncing these words in a louder voice?

What ultimately prompted the strange product that is the 2010 Missal? Can we put it down merely to an ongoing failure to honor the collegiality taught by the Second Vatican Council, a failure that allowed centralized, largely unaccountable authorities and the idiosyncratic views of a powerful few to prevail? Cardinal Medina's anti-collegial "no" to a missal approved by the episcopal conferences of the English-speaking world coincided with a 1998 *motu proprio* of John Paul II, *Ad Apostolos Suos*, which required unanimous decisions when bishops' conferences were voting on doctrinal matters. Where such unanimity is not achieved, the teaching must be referred to the Holy See for its approval or disapproval. This effectively emasculated doctrinal teaching coming from such conferences by requiring from them a higher standard than that which prevailed at Vatican II. None of the sixteen documents of the council was literally approved by every bishop; there were always a few standouts. Complete unanimity was never the case. In the late 1990s real collegiality, especially in the functioning of bishops' conferences, suffered a wintry season. Yet this is not the whole story.

Here Peter Jeffery has some valuable comments to make. Chapter 2 cited his trenchant criticism of *Liturgiam Authenticam*: "what it lacks in factuality it makes up with naked aggression. It speaks words of power and control rather than cooperation and consultation, much less charity." Despite his criticism, he ended his *Translating Tradition* with twenty pages on "Saving the Roman Rite." Behind *Liturgiam Authenticam* he detected a sincere desire for a deeper sense of the sacred, a hunger to be connected with eternal reality, and a yearning to experience the mysterious holiness of God.

This hunger fuelled the composition of the misguided 2010 Missal. Aiming at liturgical texts written in a "sacred" vernacular that came "halfway" between Latin and English was a bogus solution. It also meant forgetting that a word-centered liturgy, even one using direct, contemporary English, will not satisfy the human desire for the sacred. Liturgy is far from being essentially a matter of texts, a word-centered affair that stands or falls simply on the quality of its language. Music, sacred art, silence, the body language of presiders and assembled faithful, flowers, bells, incense, the physical layout of churches and chapels, and the quality of vestments, altars, statues, and church furniture can evoke and enhance an experience of the divine presence and love. Liturgy is a nonverbal as well as a verbal performance. Let us not forget that this wider performance also includes something described as early as the second century in the writings of St. Justin Martyr: the celebration of the Eucharist became the occasion and motivation for serving the poor and the needy.

This book has set out to show how far superior the translation found in the 1998 Missal is to that of the 2010 Missal. I have written out of a desire that the English-speaking conferences of bishops will act quickly and, by introducing the 1998 Missal, allow the presiders and congregations to celebrate the liturgy in what is truly their own language. But I also yearn for a huge leap forward in the quality of the nonverbal elements listed above. They can enrich public worship in ways that allow the powerful presence of the tripersonal God to be felt as deeply and widely as possible.

A Coda: An Open Letter to English-speaking Bishops

In the issue of March 7, 2015, the London *Tablet* published an open letter of mine to the English-speaking bishops. The favorable reception of this letter encouraged me to write a book that would plead the cause of the 1998 Missal. Let me now end this book by repeating my heartfelt request to those bishops.

> One of the great blessings of my life has come from teaching and learning from many of you when you were seminarians or young priests and took courses with me in Rome (1973–2006) and elsewhere. Some of you came to me for the sacrament of reconciliation. Many of you have invited me to lecture or lead retreats in your dioceses and welcomed me when I came. I have treasured our friendship and been encouraged by your example.

> My hope now is that you will act quickly to help English-speaking Catholics participate more effectively in the liturgy—a central recommendation in Vatican II's very first document. You all know that your bishops' conferences approved a revised translation completed after sixteen years of work by the International Commission on English in the Liturgy. You also know that the 1998 translation, when sent to the Congregation for Divine Worship and the Discipline of the Sacraments, was simply rejected without any dialogue. Roman authorities set up a commission called *Vox Clara* ("a clear voice") which was largely responsible for the "revised" translation of 2010 that came into force in November 2011. Ironically, the results produced by *Vox Clara* were too often unclear and sometimes verging on the unintelligible. The present 2010 translation regularly sounds like Latin texts transposed into English words rather than genuine English prose. A notable English writer, Monsignor Ronald Knox, like many others before and after him, wanted translations that "read like a first-rate native thing." Who could say that of our present missal? Over and over again it reads like Latin or Latin texts simply transposed into English words.

> Those who prepared the 2010 Missal aimed at a "sacral style"—something that is alien to the direct and familiar way of speaking to God and about God practiced by the psalmists and taught by Jesus. He never encouraged us to say: "graciously grant, we pray, that you give us our daily bread," or "may thy will, we pray, O Lord, be done through your prevenient grace." He asked us to pray simply and directly to God: "thy will be done; give us this day our daily bread."

What would Jesus say about the 2010 Missal? Would he approve of its clunky, Latinized English that aspires to a "sacral" style which, allegedly, will "inspire" worshipers? Many of you have copies of the "missal that wasn't," the 1998 translation summarily dismissed by the Congregation for Divine Worship. It's easily available on the internet. Set it alongside the 2010 Missal and there should be no debate about the version to choose. Like the Lord's Prayer and like the psalms, which fed the prayer life of Jesus, the 1998 translation is straightforward. As an example of genuine English, it is incomparably better than that imposed on English-speaking Catholics in November 2011. Remembering the blessing of your long-standing presence in my life, I yearn for a final blessing, a quick solution to our liturgical woes. The 1998 translation is there, waiting in the wings. Please pass on now to English-speaking Catholics the 1998 Missal that you or your predecessors originally voted for only a few years ago.

When this letter was widely and positively received, I decided to enlist the expert help of John Wilkins in writing a book. The recent decision of Pope Francis to revisit *Liturgiam Authenticam*, which provided faulty guidelines for what became the 2010 Missal, gives us hope that this papal initiative may lead to the 2010 Missal being dropped and the 1998 Missal being finally introduced—to the immense benefit of English-speaking Catholics around the world.

I finish by thanking John Wilkins very warmly. He has contributed a chapter (chap. 1) and edited the whole book.

Postscript: September 2017[1]

*I*n a diary kept during the Second Vatican Council, Yves Congar, the leading figure among all the theological *periti* (experts), every now and then expressed his outrage. Reacting to the announcement that certain powers were to be "given" to the bishops, he wrote: "Over the centuries these powers were *stolen* from the bishops. They are being *given back* what was stolen from them!"

Pope Francis in a *motu proprio* or personal edict of 3 September 2017, which brings corresponding amendments to canon 838 of the Code of Canon Law, has just given back to the national conferences of bishops the responsibility for liturgical *translations*, which had been stolen from them after the Council. His very first words point to the theft that occurred: "The important principle [*Magnum Principium*], confirmed by the Second Vatican Council, according to which the liturgical prayer, adapted to the comprehension of the people, can be understood, has required the serious task, entrusted to the bishops, of introducing the vernacular into the liturgy and of preparing and approving versions of the liturgical books." In short, the task of preparing and approving *translations* rightly belongs to the local bishops, as Vatican II mandated, and not to any group or office of the Holy See.

In *Magnum Principium*, after hearing the views of a commission of bishops and experts he appointed at the end of 2016, Pope Francis

---

[1] As *Lost in Translation* was about to be printed, Pope Francis published a personal edict (a *motu proprio*) that is highly relevant to this book. With permission, we present here an abbreviated version of the article Gerald O'Collins wrote (and John Wilkins edited) for the London *Tablet* (September 16, 2017).

has recalled from Vatican II the "right" of all "the faithful of whatever age and culture" to "share in a conscious and active way in the liturgical celebrations." This calls for translations that are not only faithful to the Latin original but also intelligible when they are proclaimed in the vernacular languages. Without naming *Comme le Prévoit* or *Liturgiam Authenticam*, the pope instructs translators to follow such guidelines where they continue to prove "useful"—a polite way of implying that *Liturgiam Authenticam* no longer enjoys authoritative status. He then shows his preference for the "meaning-for-meaning" translation encouraged by *Comme le Prévoit* rather than the "word-for-word" approach enjoined by *Liturgiam Authenticam.*

The necessary "fidelity" of translations, the pope writes, "cannot always be judged by individual words" but "in the context of the whole act of communication." That is to say, translators should render "fully and faithfully the *meaning* of the original text" (emphasis added) and preserve "the *native character* of each language." Here Pope Francis stands shoulder to shoulder with the views of translation proposed by St. Jerome, St. Thomas Aquinas, and other authorities in the history of Christianity.

In a letter to Pope Urban IV, Aquinas wrote: "It is the task of a good translator, when translating material dealing with the Catholic faith, to preserve the meaning but to adapt the mode of expression, so that it is in harmony with the idiom of the language into which he is translating." Aquinas rejected a word-for-word in favor of a meaning-for-meaning translation: "When anything expressed in one language is translated merely word-for-word into another, it will be no surprise if perplexity concerning the meaning of the original sometimes occurs."

In *Magnum Principium*, Pope Francis recalls "the difficulties" that have arisen "between the bishops' conferences and the Apostolic See." There is need for "collaboration full of mutual trust"—a courteous way of telling the CDW to show due respect to the authority of bishops' conferences.

The ball is now firmly in the court of the English-speaking bishops' conferences. The excellent 1998 translation is there, waiting in the wings. A few additions need to be made: to include, for instance, the new feasts and memorials of saints introduced from the late 1990s. But substantially the bishops already have what they need to make the Roman Missal once again a comprehensible and powerful tool of evangelization when people experience it. Any episcopal conference, for example, the New Zealand bishops' conference, which is well aware of the defective nature of the 2010 Missal, could submit to the CDW for confirmation the 1998 Missal that their predecessors had already approved. If so, I respectfully suggest that they might also send a letter to Pope Francis to thank him for his *motu proprio* and explain how they are putting into practice what he has just decreed.Index of Names

Select Bibliography

Baldovin, John F. "Idols and Icons: Reflections on the Current State of Liturgical Reform." *Worship* 84 (2010): 386–402.

Duffy, Eamon. "Lay Appropriation of the Sacraments in the Later Middle Ages." *New Blackfriars* 77 (1996): 53–68.

Finn, Peter C., and James M. Schellman, eds. *Shaping English Liturgy*. Washington, DC: Pastoral Press, 1990.

Foley, Edward, gen. ed. *A Commentary on the Order of Mass of the Roman Missal*. Collegeville, MN: Liturgical Press, 2011.

Francis, Mark, and Keith Pecklers, eds. *Liturgy for the New Millennium: A Commentary on the Revised Sacramentary*. Collegeville, MN: Liturgical Press, 2000.

Harbert, Bruce. *Companion to the Order of Mass: The New Translation*. London: Catholic Truth Society, 2011.

———. "What Kind of Missal Are We Getting?" *New Blackfriars* 77 (1996): 548–52.

ICEL. *Documents on the Liturgy 1963–1979: Conciliar, Papal and Curial Texts*. Collegeville, MN: Liturgical Press, 1982.

———. *Shaping English Liturgy: Studies in Honor of Archbishop Denis Hurley*. Washington, DC: Pastoral Press, 1990.

———. *Opening Prayers: Scripture-related Collects for Years A, B & C from the Sacramentary*. Norwich: Canterbury Press, 1999.

Jeffery, Peter. *Translating Tradition: A Chant Historian Reads* Liturgiam Authenticam. Collegeville, MN: Liturgical Press, 2005.

Johnson, Clare V. "Paradigms of Translation." *Worship* 77 (2003): 151–70.

Johnson, Cuthbert. *Understanding the Roman Missal: The New Translation*. London: Catholic Truth Society, 2011.

Johnson, Maxwell E. "Liturgy and Ecumenism: Gifts, Challenges, and Hopes for a Renewed Vision." *Worship* 80 (2006): 2–29.

————. "The Loss of a Common Language: The End of Ecumenical Liturgical Convergence." *Studia Liturgica* 37 (2007): 55–72.

Jungmann, Josef. *The Mass of the Roman Rite: Its Origins and Development.* New York: Benziger, 1959.

Kearney, Paddy, ed. *Memories: Memoirs of Archbishop Denis E. Hurley, O.M.I.* Pietermaritzburg, South Africa: Cluster Publications, 2000.

Krosnicki, Thomas A. "Opening Prayers for Lent: Forty-Four Plus One." *Worship* 88 (2014): 119–36.

Larson, Jan P. "A Case for Changing Liturgical Words." *Worship* 86 (2012): 60–70.

Magas, Kevin D. "Issues in Eucharistic Praying: Translating the Roman Canon." *Worship* 89 (2015): 482–505.

Marini, Piero. *A Challenging Reform: Realizing the Vision of Liturgical Renewal.* Dublin: Columba Press, 2007.

Martin, James, ed. *Celebrating Good Liturgies: A Guide to the Ministries of the Mass.* Chicago: Loyola Press, 2005.

Moore, Gerard. *Vatican II and the Collects for Ordinary Time: A Study in the Roman Missal (1975).* San Francisco: International Scholars Publications, 1998.

Nichols, Bridget, ed. *The Collect in the Churches of the Reformation.* London: SCM Press, 2012.

O'Loughlin, Thomas. "The Liturgical Vessels of the Latin Eucharistic Liturgy: A Case of an Embedded Theology." *Worship* 82 (2008): 482–504.

Pecklers, Keith. *Dynamic Equivalence: The Living Language of Christian Worship.* Collegeville, MN: Liturgical Press, 2003.

Ramshaw, Gail. "Wording the Sanctus: A Case Study in Liturgical Language." *Worship* 77 (2003): 325–40.

Regan, Patrick. *Advent to Pentecost: Comparison of the Seasons in the Ordinary and Extraordinary Forms of the Roman Rite.* Collegeville, MN: Liturgical Press, 2012.

Reid, Alcuin, ed. *Liturgy in the Twenty-First Century: Contemporary Issues and Perspectives.* New York: Bloomsbury, 2016.

Ryan, Michael G. "Why Pope Francis Is Right to Revisit the New Mass Translation." *America,* January 27, 2017.

Seasoltz, R. Kevin. "The Genius of the Roman Rite. On the Reception and Implementation of the New Missal." *Worship* 83 (2009): 541–49.

Taft, Robert. "On Translating Liturgically." *Logos: A Journal of Eastern Christian Studies* 39 (1998): 155–84.

Trautman, Donald W. "The Relationship of the Active Participation of the Assembly to Liturgical Translations." *Worship* 80 (2006): 290–309.

Turner, Paul. *Glory in the Cross: Holy Week in the Third Edition of the Roman Missal.* Collegeville, MN: Liturgical Press, 2011.

Wigan, Bernard, ed. *The Liturgy in English.* London: Oxford University Press, 1962.

Wilson, George B. "Liturgical Governance: From Vatican II to the New Roman Missal." *Worship* 87 (2013): 245–99.

Index of Names